Studies in 20th Cen...

Ge...

For James Ernest Marshall 1913–1982

Acknowledgements

The author would like to thank the following for their help:

Scott Harrison, Ann Usborne, Bill Osborne and Steve Ogden

The publishers would like to thank the following for permission to reproduce photographs:

Archives du Centre de Documentation Juive Contemporaine, p. 36; Gunn Brinson, pp. 11 (top right), 46 (right), 47 bottom; Bundesarchiv, pp. 17, 19; Colorific/Hugo Jaeger, pp. 29, 44 (top right), 51 (left), 54 (bottom), 77; The Anne Frank Foundation, p. 35; Nicholas Garland/*The Independent*, p. 78 (right); John Hillelson, pp. 8 (top right), 27 (left); The Robert Hunt Library, pp. 16, 28, 31, 33 (bottom), 38, 39, 42, 59, 60 (top), 62, 64, 68, 69 (top and bottom left), 70 (bottom left and right), 71 (right), 74 (left); Imperial War Museum, pp. 43, 66 (right), 67 (left); International Institute for Social History, pp. 21, 44 (top left); David King, pp. 27 (right), 34, 45, 46 (left), 47, 49; from Stefan Lorant's *Sieg Heil*, an illustrated history of Germany from Bismarck to Hitler (Authors Edition, Lenox, pp. 8 (bottom right), 9 (bottom right), 11 (top left); David Low/Centre for the Study of Cartoons and Caricature, Canterbury, p. 25; Moro Roma, pp. 4, 7, 12, 40 (right); Popperfoto, pp. 65 (left), 67 (right), 70 (top left), 71 (left), 72 (left), 73, 75, 76 (left); Süddeutscher Verlag, pp. 5, 6, 13, 14, 32, 33 (top), 40 (left), 44 (bottom left), 50, 51 (right), 54 (top), 55, 76 (right), 78 (left), 80; Topham Picture Library, pp. 23 (bottom), 26, 52, 58, 63; Ullstein, pp. 53, 56, 57, 60 (bottom), 61, 65 (right), 66 (left), 69 (bottom right), 72 (right), 74 (right); U.S. National Archives, p. 22; The Wiener Library, pp. 8 (left and top right), 9 (left), 10, 11 (bottom), 23 (top), 30, 37, 44 (top left).

Oxford University Press, Walton Street, Oxford OX2 6DP

Oxford New York Toronto
Delhi Bombay Calcutta Madras Karachi
Petaling Jaya Singapore Hong Kong Tokyo
Nairobi Dar es Salaam Cape Town
Melbourne Auckland

and associated companies in
Berlin Ibadan

Oxford is a trademark of Oxford University Press

© Oxford University Press 1989

First published in 1989

Reprinted in 1992

ISBN 0 19 913333 6

Typesetting by MS Filmsetting Limited, Frome, Somerset
Printed in Hong Kong

Oxford University Press

Studies in 20th Century World History

Introduction

This series is designed to confront the principal objectives of GCSE history and to provide practical schemes of work which include sources of historical evidence, questions, and mark schemes.

Several assumptions underpin the series. Firstly, evidence is seen to be at the heart of historical study. The evidence in this book comes from a wide range of sources. Each chapter is a unique combination of sources selected to encapsulate, as far as possible, an aspect of the work of the historian. Whereas this book cannot claim to enable students to pursue an exhaustive study of available evidence, the evidence has been selected to provide breadth and balance within the scope of each exercise.

Secondly, the evidence has been selected with a particular historical skill in mind. It will be seen that each chapter is double-headed. The whole book covers sixteen major topics of German history, but at the same time uses the individual material of each of these chapters to pursue a particular historical objective. At the end of each chapter can be found questions which meet the coursework requirements of GCSE examining boards.

Content has often been undervalued in the recent historical debate. This series shows how skills and content can complement each other to produce effective and highly motivated learning in history.

Contents

Chapter 1 Versailles and Weimar: The stab in the back? 4
A study of facts and judgements

Chapter 2 The depression in Germany 7
An exercise in the interpretation and evaluation of visual evidence

Chapter 3 The Münich Putsch 12
A study of the problems of using secondary evidence

Chapter 4 The Reichstag fire 16
An exercise in historical reasoning and inference

Chapter 5 The Night of the Long Knives 22
A study in causation and motivation

Chapter 6 Propaganda 26
An exercise in the reliability and usefulness of primary evidence

Chapter 7 The Nazi Police State 32
An exercise in the interpretation of primary evidence

Chapter 8 Holocaust 35
An exercise in the use and evaluation of fiction, autobiography and diaries as historical evidence

Chapter 9 The Hitler Youth 43
A study of a movement and its influence

Chapter 10 The German economy under the Nazis 49
An exercise in the interpretation and analysis of evidence

Chapter 11 Opposition and appeasement: 1938 53
A study in the analysis of historical narrative

Chapter 12 Rommel 58
A study of the role of the individual

Chapter 13 The Atlantic War 63
An exercise in the synthesis of an historical account

Chapter 14 Barbarossa: The invasion of Russia 1941 68
A study in cause and consequence

Chapter 15 The last days of Adolf Hitler 74
An exercise in the comparison of historical evidence

Chapter 16 Austria: past and present 77
A study of the current situation in the context of past events

Chapter 1 Versailles and Weimar:

The stab in the back?

A study of facts and judgements

In September 1918, people in Germany didn't realise how badly the war was going. Although German troops had inflicted heavy casualties on them, the Allies were still moving forward. On Germany's side both Turkey and Bulgaria were facing defeat and ready to negotiate for peace. Once they had surrendered, Germany's south eastern flank was undefended. No German troops from the west could be spared to reinforce it.

Even though no foreign troops were on German soil, General Ludendorff realised that all was lost and urged the government to seek a peace settlement, but without making his action known to the army or the German public. Reluctantly they appealed to President Wilson of the USA, to negotiate the terms for ending the war. News of these negotiations caused final German resistance to collapse. On 9 November the Kaiser fled to Holland where he abdicated. A Republic was proclaimed in Berlin.

The new German government took over and began its rule at Weimar in February 1919 and faced its first responsibility to settle the war.

A From *Years of Change* by R. Wolfson, 1978.

In November 1918 the Germans had had the better of the four years of fighting. In the East the Russians had been beaten and surrendered enormous amounts of territory. In the West the German front line was still in enemy territory when they asked for peace. Her losses were less than those of her enemies. She surrendered not because she had been defeated, but because she knew that she would be. The future was hopeless for Germany. The entry of the United States had not made an impact but the potential of America's contribution was enormous. ... As important was the economic decline in Germay itself ... the result of the British blockade. German agriculture was hit disastrously by the war ... the conscription of agricultural workers ... rationing. How could her people keep up their morale and enthusiasm for the war through another winter?

B Kaiser William II, speaking to military leaders on 11 August 1918:

> We have nearly reached the limit of our powers of resistance. The war must be ended.

Hitler is on the left in this photograph taken at battalion headquarters near the front line at Ypres

C *Hitler was a messenger during the war and won two Iron Crosses for bravery. Here he is seen (on the left) with a fellow soldier in an infantry regiment*

D From *Mein Kampf* by Adolf Hitler, 1925. Hitler wrote this book whilst in prison for trying to seize power in 1923. It contained most of his personal beliefs and ideas. Referring to the end of the war in 1918, he said:

Since I had stood at my mother's grave I had not wept ... now I could not help it ... all personal suffering vanishes in comparison with the misfortunes of the fatherland ... so it all had been in vain ... all the sacrifices ... the hunger and thirst ... the shame of indignation and disgrace burned my brow. In these nights hatred grew in me, hatred for those responsible for this deed. ...

Kaiser William II held out the hand of friendship to the leaders of Marxism, without suspecting that the scoundrels have no honour. While they still held the Imperial hand in theirs, their own hand was reaching for the dagger. There is no making pacts with Jews.

E From *The King's depart – The tragedy of Germany: Versailles and the German Revolution* by R. Watt, 1969.

A belief was beginning to sweep through the officer corps that it had been the victim of a 'Dolchstoss', a 'stab in the back', by certain faithless and cowardly citizens. Had it not been for this, the German army would have won the war.

The Socialists made little effort to counteract the tale even though they would receive the lion's share of the blame ... with the result that the officer corps were provided with a grievance which, when added to the provisions of the peace treaty were more than enough to convince the army that it was the victim of treachery by the civil government.

F From The Treaty of Versailles, 28 June 1919.

Article 231
The Allied Governments affirm [state] and Germany accepts the responsibility for causing all loss and damage to which the allied governments have been subjected as a consequence of the war imposed upon them by the aggression of Germany.

Article 232
The Allied Governments require and Germany undertakes that she will make compensation for all damage done.

G From *From Vienna to Versailles* by L. C. B. Seaman, 1955.

As for the 'war guilt' clause ... it is difficult to see what were the objections to it. ... In whatever sense the word 'responsibility' is taken, to apply it to Germany and her Allies is to state historical fact.

The clause stimulated a number of Historians inside and outside Germany to try to prove that the war was really the fault of the French or the Russians or Sir Edward Grey or armaments manufacturers or the balance of power or so forth but by now there is no need to take such attempts seriously.

H From *The Origins of the Second World War* by A. J. P. Taylor, 1963.

... the great problem which had caused the war still lay at the centre of international affairs when the war ended ... it was the place of Germany which was in dispute. The study of war origins had an urgent and practical importance. ... Historians laboured to show that the allied governments were a good deal guiltier and the Germans more innocent than the peace-makers of 1919 supposed. The rights and wrongs of these controversies, international and domestic, ... no longer matter.

I *A huge crowd celebrated the outbreak of war in Munich on 1 August, 1914. In it was Adolf Hitler (ringed)*

Questions
1. Read Source **D**. Who does Hitler blame for Germany's defeat? 3
2. Compare Sources **D** and **E**.
   a) On what points do sources **D** and **E** agree? 2
   b) Would you describe the views expressed in each document as fact, opinion or judgement? Explain your answer. 7
3. 'Hitler must have gained popularity because he was saying what all Germans felt about their defeat'. How likely is this judgement to be true? 2
4. Look at Source **F**. Why does Article 232 depend on and follow Article 231? 6
5. Read Sources **F**, **G** and **H**. At the time, why did the historians's work matter? 4
6. Refer to any of the sources. Was the 'stab in the back' fact or opinion? Explain your answer carefully. 6

Chapter 2 The depression in Germany

An exercise in the interpretation and evaluation of visual evidence

When the First World War ended, it left the German people broken and half-starved. The harvest in 1918 was disastrous and the rate of exchange was about 20 marks to the pound (sterling). By the time of the worst inflation in late 1923, the rate was 20 000 *million* marks to the pound. Wages were collected daily, often in wheelbarrows. The price of a cup of coffee could double in the time it took to drink it.

The Versailles Treaty took away from Germany some of her most important reserves of iron ore and coal. Germany also had to find the money to rebuild her shattered industry. On top of all these problems, the Allies wanted compensating for their losses and suffering in the war. A grand total of 132 million marks or about £11 million was expected as reparations. In 1923 when reparations payments were not being met, French and Belgian forces occupied the Ruhr district and tried to force payment. The Germans reacted with a policy of passive resistance and non-cooperation. This reduced production and ultimately cost German industry twice as much as the annual reparations payments.

Some historians have blamed the German government for not balancing the budget and for issuing more and more money which they did not have. Other historians say that the problems of the German economy were impossible to solve and the government was only partly to blame. In 1924 America tried to solve the problem of reparations by reducing the amount to be paid and increasing the number of payments so that each one was smaller. Also large loans were made to Germany. These measures were known as the Dawes plan.

The consequences varied for different sections of the community. Wage-earners became poorer but the greatest revolution was suffered by the middle class who depended on their salaries and income from the investment of their private savings, which were now virtually wiped out. It was a most appalling blow for the most stable element of society and it was eventually to cost the Weimar Republic dear. Thousands became destitute, and from their despair the Communist and Nazi parties were later to draw powerful support.

Ten years after the beginning of the First World War. This illustration gives an idea of the atmosphere that led to the birth of Nazism

A *The Milk Profiteer – 'Ah well, big profits require small sacrifices'. May 1920.*

B *Paper money! Paper money! Bread! Bread! June 1923.*

C *Berliners search through ash piles for usable pieces of coal.*

D *Currency speculators remember the hungry children! December 1921.*

E *A woman exchanges a whole packet of marks for one American dollar. The German currency collapsed in 1921.*

F *Middle-class women sell tin cans to help keep their families going.*

G *December 1920 – in Berlin.*

H *December 1920 – in the German countryside.*

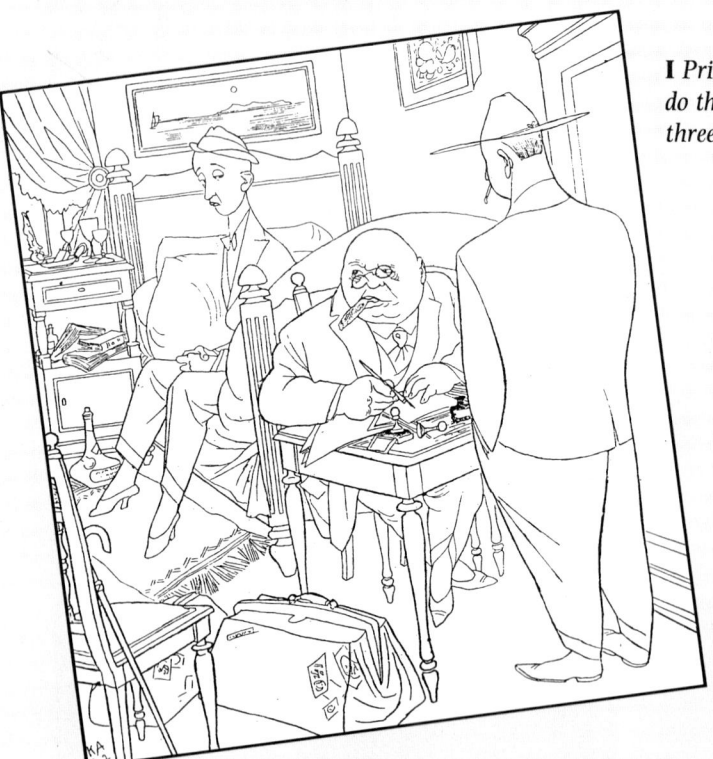

I *Private passport office – 'This time little Reinhold will do the jewellers. You've already been over the border three times'. May 1922.*

J *From left: Take another good Havana with you, before I shut up shop!; Genuine English toilet soap! Wonderfully fragrant!; Mucki, Schnucki, the darling of the ladies, the pleasure of the men! Fantastic French race!; Pst!. October 1919.*

K *A defenceless old man is approached by a French soldier. A German photograph showing French behaviour in the Ruhr.*

L *A German illustration entitled 'French heroes in the Ruhr'.*

M *An early NSDAP election poster. The main title says 'First bread, then reparations'.*

Questions

1. **a)** Refer to the pictures and photographs **A–H** and the background information. What is the artist trying to say about Germany in 1920? **5**
   b) Do the photographs support or contradict what is in the pictures? **5**
2. Refer to picture **K** and the background information. How might this photograph be seen as propaganda? **4**
3. Refer to **A, B, D, I** and **J**. What do these cartoons tell us about German trade and industry after the war? **6**
4. Study, Source **M**, closely. How could the Nazis use the economic situation to their advantage? **4**
5. Consider the cartoons and the photographs. What is the value of each type of source to the historian of Weimar Germany? Illustrate your answer by reference to the sources. **6**

Chapter 3 The Munich Putsch

A study of the problems of using secondary evidence

After the First World War Hitler joined the German Workers party as an education officer. With Hitler's gift of speech-making the party grew in numbers. In February 1920 it became the National Socialist German Workers Party. In the following year Hitler became its leader.

In this chapter you will look mainly at the work of three historical writers: an English historian, Alan Bullock (1952); a German historian, Joachim Fest (1973); and an American journalist, John Dornberg (1982). Each writer describes and explains an important event in Hitler's early career – the Munich Putsch.

The Nazis, as the party had become known, were not interested in parliamentary power, they were a form of military organisation. They aimed to start a violent uprising, called a putsch, in which they would seize power from the socialist Weimar government. The Nazis attracted many men with military experience, who formed a bodyguard for Hitler – the SA. Hitler also had the support of a famous old First World War hero – General Ludendorff.

Hitler began his putsch in a Munich beer hall by interrupting the leader of the state government – Baron von Kahr, in the middle of his speech. As you will read, what happened in the beer hall is not clear. Hitler spent a long time trying to persuade Kahr to help him start a revolution from Munich that would sweep through the Germany. Kahr seemed to support Hitler. When he left the beer hall Kahr immediately made plans to stop the Nazis and he alerted the police to be ready for Hitler's march through Munich. The next day the march was halted at the Odeonplatz, the police faced up to the marchers. Someone fired a shot. No one to this day is sure who fired the first shot – the Nazis or the Police. There was a brief but fierce exchange of gunfire between the Nazis and the police.

When the firing started there was great confusion. Hitler and Ludendorff reacted in different ways. What happened to Hitler has caused the most disagreement amongst historians.

Hitler's membership card of the German Workers Party

What happened in the Munich beer hall?

A The words of A. Otto von Muller, eyewitness, 8 November 1923:

> Herr Kahr had spoken for half an hour. Then there was movement at the entrance as if people were wanting to push their way in ... I saw Hitler emerge between two armed soldiers ... Hitler climbed on a chair on my left ... then Hitler made a sign to the man on his right, who fired a shot at the ceiling ... Hitler called out (I cannot recollect the exact order of his words), 'The National Revolution has broken out. The hall is surrounded.' Maybe he mentioned the exact number. I am not sure ...

B From *Hitler: A Study in Tyranny* by A. Bullock, 1952.

Hitler took up an inconspicuous position by one of the pillars ... no one paid any attention to him ... Twenty minutes after Kahr had begun to speak, Goering, with 25 Brownshirts, burst into the hall. In the middle of the uproar Hitler leaped onto a chair and fired a shot at the ceiling then jumped down and began to push his way onto the platform, 'The National Revolution has begun,' he shouted, 'this hall is occupied by 600 heavily armed men. No one may leave the hall.'

C From *Hitler* by J. Fest, 1973.

Kahr was well into his speech when Hitler appeared at the door ... According to eyewitness accounts, he was extremely agitated ... Hitler held up a beer glass and as a heavy machine gun appeared at his side, he took a dramatic swallow, smashed the glass to the floor and with a pistol in his raised hand stormed into the middle of the hall at the head of an armed squad. Glasses crashed to the floor and chairs toppled. Hitler leaped onto a table, fired his famous shot into the ceiling to catch the crowd's attention and forced his way through the dumbfounded throng to the platform, 'The National Revolution has begun,' he cried, 'the hall is surrounded by 600 heavily armed men. No one may leave the premises.'

Members of the SA on the way to Munich for Hitler's putsch of 9 November 1923

D *An artist's impression of the beer hall (1933).*

Who fired the first shot during the march?

E From *An official police report for the committee of enquiry*, 1924.

> ... police officers were spat upon, ... pistols with safety catches off were stuck in their chests. The police used rubber truncheons and rifle butts to push back the crowd. Suddenly, a National Socialist fired a pistol at police officer and killed a sergeant ... before it was possible to give an order the comrades of the sergeant opened fire as the Hitler lot did. A short gun battle followed.

F From *Hitler: a study in tyranny* by A. Bullock, 1952.

Hitler shouted, 'Surrender!'. At this moment a shot rang out and a hail of bullets swept the street. The shooting lasted only half a minute ... 16 Nazis and three police lay dead or dying ... All was confusion.

G From *Hitler* by J. Fest, 1973.

What happened is not exactly clear ... [there is] agreement on only one point: a single shot rang out, provoking a steady exchange of fire ... [of] about 60 seconds ... when it was all over, 14 members of the procession and three policemen lay dead or dying on the street, ... many others had been wounded.

H From *The Putsch that failed* by J. Dornberg, 1982.

Who fired the shot has never been clarified ... the police insisted afterwards that it came from the demonstrators ranks. Adolf Lenk insists the first shot came from the 'police line' ... it killed his friend Kurt, blowing half his head away.

Witnesses said the first shot came from neither side but from the roof or high window of the Preysing Palace. A sniper? A Provocateur? An Army Lieutenant and a Sergeant both heard a retort and saw smoke from a window. Godin [Police Lieutenant] later sent one of his men into the building to investigate. Empty shell casings and powder burns were found on a number of window sills.

Was Hitler a coward or a hero?

I From *Hitler: a study in tyranny* by A. Bullock, 1952.

Hitler fell, either pulled down or seeking cover. One man alone kept his head. Ludendorff marched steadily on, pushed through the line of police ... the situation might have been saved but not a single man followed him. Hitler at the critical moment lost his nerve. According to eyewitnesses, one of them a National Socialist – Dr. Schulz and Dr. Gebhard – Hitler was the first to scramble to his feet and stumbling back towards the end of the procession, allowed himself to be pushed by Schulz into a yellow motorcar ... Worst of all from Hitler's point of view was the contrast between his own behaviour under fire and that of Ludendorff.

J From *Hitler* by J. Fest, 1973.

Richter fatally wounded, in his fall pulled Hitler with him, wrenching his arm out of joint. Amidst the hail of bullets, while all were dropping to the ground or scurrying for cover, Ludendorff stalked upright, trembling with rage through the Police cordon. The day might possibly have ended differently had a small band of determined men followed him: but no one did. Hitler scrambled up from the pavement and took to his heels leaving behind him the dead and the wounded. In the midst of the general chaos he managed to escape with the help of an ambulance. A few years later he concocted the legend that he had carried a child out of the firing line to safety; he even produced the child.

K From *The Putsch that failed* by J. Dornberg 1982.

Many of the wounded did not wait for help. Instead they made their escape to avoid falling into police hands – especially the leaders.

Hitler was first. Max Kronauer pulled him from under Richter's body and helped him struggle painfully to his feet. Dr Schulz hurried towards him and led him through the fleeing panic-stricken mob toward the yellow Opel. On the way they came upon a ten year old boy – an innocent spectator – Gottfried Mayr – lying at the curb and bleeding profusely from a bullet wound in the upper arm. At Hitler's suggestion, Schulz and a cousin-in-law, a Munich student, took the youth along to the car and hastily gave him first aid.

Questions

1. Read Sources **A**, **B** and **C**.
   a) Make a list of the things about which these sources disagree. 4
   b) Why do you think that there are such differences? Give your reasons. 7
   c) Consider the picture Source **D** carefully. Explain how the impression created by Source **D** is different from the accounts in Sources **A**, **B** and **C**? 7
2. Source **C** says that it is based on eyewitness accounts like Source **A**. Yet Muller (Source **A**) admits that he cannot remember exactly. Should we doubt the reliability of Source **A** or **C** or both? 4
3. How does the style of writing used in **C** differ from the style of **A** or **B**? 3
4. Read Source **E**. It was written at the time and clearly states who fired the first shot. Why do you think that none of the historians accept this account? 6
5. Is there any point in studying what happened in the beer hall and on the march if the historians disagree so much? 5
6. Compare Sources **I** and **J** in the way they describe Hitler and Ludendorff's behaviour after the shooting started.
   a) Are they reporting the facts or making judgements? 4
   b) Was it important to know how Hitler behaved? 7
7. Source **K** was written after Source **J** but accepts the story of Hitler helping a child to safety. Why might this be so? 5
8. The author of Source **K** is not a historian but a trained journalist. When he was a young child, Dornberg's family suffered persecution under the Nazis. He and his family left Germany to find refuge in the United States, where he grew up. Would his background affect his historical writing? Give your reasons. 8

Chapter 4 The Reichstag fire

An exercise in historical reasoning and inference

On 27 February 1933 the German Parliament building, the Reichstag, burnt down. Marinus van der Lubbe, a young Dutchman, with Communist connections, was caught red-handed lighting fires in the building. The Nazis used this as a justification for arresting the leaders of the Communist Party. The day after the fire Hindenberg was persuaded, by Hitler, to sign an emergency decree 'for the protection of people and state'. This removed a German citizen's normal right to a trial if arrested. The Nazi dictatorship had begun.

The timing of the fire was very convenient for the Nazis in the run-up to elections in March 1933. The Communists lost seats (from 100 down to 81) and the Nazis won 288, with support from other right wing groups; this was a crucial majority.

The Nazis put van der Lubbe on trial in Leipzig in 1933. No connection between van der Lubbe and the Communists who were rounded up after the fire could be found and they were cleared.

Suspicion then fell upon the Nazis themselves because they seemed to have benefited from the fire politically. Had they deliberately planned the blaze to discredit the Communists? Communists outside Germany held their own mock trial in Paris in 1934, except this time the Nazis stood accused. The Communists hoped to gain great publicity from the event.

In this chapter you will be able to consider for yourself the evidence that suggested that it was the Nazis themselves who set fire to the Reichstag. However remember that throughout the first trial, the most consistent evidence was that of Marinus van der Lubbe who never changed his statement.

A *Flames light up the dome of the Reichstag as it burns on the night of 27 February 1933.*

B From van der Lubbe's statement to Police, 3 March 1933.

... my action was inspired by political motives. I have always followed German politics with keen interest. When Hitler took over ... I expected much enthusiasm for him but also much tension ... I was a member of the Communist Party until 1929. I did not like the way they [the Communist leaders] lord it over the workers, instead of letting the workers decide for themselves.

    I decided to go to Germany to see for myself. I made the decision and came to Germany all by myself ... a system which grants freedom to one side and metes out oppression to the other ... something had to be done in protest. Since the workers would do nothing, I had to do something by myself. I considered arson a suitable method. I did not wish to harm private people but something that belonged to the system itself ... I acted alone ... No one at all helped me, nor did I meet a single person in the Reichstag.

C *The gutted remains of the Reichstag on the morning of 28 February 1933. At the time it was thought that a fire big enough and fierce enough to have caused this destruction could not have been started by one man.*

The case against the Nazis

D The 'Confession' of Karl Ernst. Ernst was killed in the 'Night of the Long Knives'. This confession was part of the evidence published in Paris in 1934 by Communists. Koestler (author of Source O) helped 'find' some of this evidence.

I hereby declare that, on February 27, 1933, I and two SA men [Heines and Schultz], set fire to the German Reichstag. We did so in the belief that we would be serving the Führer and our movement....

I suggested to Goering that we use the underground passage leading from his residence to the Reichstag, because that would cut down the risk of discovery. Goebbels insisted on postponing the fire from 25 to 27, because February 26 was a Sunday, a day on which no evening papers appeared so that the fire could not be used well for propaganda purposes. We decided to start the fire at about 9 p.m., in time for quite a number of radio bulletins. Goering and Goebbels agreed on how to throw suspicion on the Communists ... during one inspection of the passage we were almost caught ...

Helldorf told us that a young fellow had turned up in Berlin of whom we could make use. This Dutch Communist, van der Lubbe, would climb into the Reichstag and blunder about conspicuously. Meanwhile I and my men would set fire to the Chamber.

The main difficulty was keeping to a precise timetable. The Dutchman was made to learn the plan of the whole Reichstag ... To make certain that van der Lubbe would not take fright or change his mind at the last moment, Sander would not leave his side all afternoon. He would escort him and watch him climb in from a safe distance. Van der Lubbe was to be left in the belief that he was working by himself.

I met my two helpers at 8 p.m. precisely. We synchronized our watches. We were all dressed in civilian clothes. In a few minutes we were at the entrance to Goering's residence. We slipped into the passage unnoticed. Hanfstaengl had diverted the watchman. At about eight o'clock we reached the dead-end branch. Here we had to wait until 8.40 p.m., i.e. until the guard had finished his round. Then we pulled galoshes over our shoes and walked on. We entered the Session Chamber at 8.45 p.m.

We prepared a number of fires by smearing chairs and tables with phosphorus mixture and by soaking carpets and curtains in paraffin. At exactly 9.05 p.m. we had finished, and started back. At 9.15 we were in the boiler-house and at 9.15 we climbed across the wall.

I have served the Führer for eleven years, and I shall remain faithful to him unto death. I cannot bear the thought that the SA was betrayed by those it helped to bring to power. The Führer will destroy the dark plotters against the SA I am writing this confession as my only insurance against the evil plans of Goering and Goebbels. I shall destroy it the moment these traitors have been paid out.

Karl Ernst, SA Gruppenführer.
Berlin, 3 June, 1934.

Addendum: This document may only be published on my orders ... or if I die a violent death.

E From *The Voice of Destruction* by H. Rauschning, 1940, New York. Rauschning a Nazi official left the Party in 1934. In the USA he published *The Voice of Destruction* which rapidly became a world-wide best-seller; it told of Hitler's intimate thoughts.

Laughter, cynical jokes, boasting were expressed by the conspirators, Goering described how 'the boys' had entered the Reichstag by an underground passage ... they had only a few minutes ... and were nearly discovered. He regretted that the 'whole shack' had not burnt down. They had been so hurried that they could not 'make of proper job of it'.

F From an entry in Goebbels' diary for 31 January 1933.

During discussions with the Führer we drew up the plans of battle against the red terror. For the time being, we decided against any direct countermeasures. The Bolshevik rebellion must first of all flare up; only then shall we hit back.

G *Van der Lubbe's trial in progress.*

The case in defence of the Nazis

H At van der Lubbe's trial by the Nazis Dr Sack was the Nazi lawyer defending the Communist, Torgler, one of the people rounded up after the fire. As his client's innocence emerged, Dr Sack took the opportunity to defend the Nazis on whom suspicion seemed to be falling.

> It is ridiculous to suggest that the Nazis should have picked a tramp as the best person to carry out a plan whose discovery would threaten the whole nation ... allowed [him] to wander about alone, in rags, begging for food, and sleeping in public shelters ... Only a fool would have instructed van der Lubbe to scale up the wall of the Reichstag, break windows ... risk discovery. This plan, allegedly invented by Goebbels, master of the art of propaganda, would have been so full of flaws as to invite discovery deliberately.

I From *City Lawyer* by A. Hayes, 1942.

Heines, the SA chief, ... presented an unimpeachable alibi. Not only he, but his wife, a nurse who attended his children, and others, testified to his whereabouts on the night of the fire, in a distant city, Gleiwitz. More convincing were newspaper clippings showing that Heines made a speech at a public meeting on February 27.

J From Herr Wingurth's evidence at van der Lubbe's trial. Wingurth was a locksmith.

> As for the underground passage ... the whole thing strikes me as extremely unlikely, because too many doors would have had to be opened and shut, and I was told that all the doors were found properly locked after the fire.

K Sefton Delmar, *Daily Express* correspondent, said in a letter to *Der Spiegel*, 25 November 1959:

> That evening, Hitler himself was not absolutely certain that the fire was a Communist plot... as we walked side by side through the burning building, 'God grant that this be the work of the Communists'... When von Papen appeared, Hitler seized his hand, with much enthusiasm, and said: This is a God-given signal, Herr Vice-Chancellor! If this fire, as I believe, is the work of the Communists, then we must crush out this murder pest with an iron fist.... what I saw of Hitler's and Goebbel's behaviour in the Reichstag does not fit in with the theory that both were party or even privy to the Reichstag fire plot.

L Rudolf Giels, Chief of Police, recalled Hitler's reaction to the fire:

> On a balcony stood Hitler... gazing at the red ocean of fire. Hitler swung round towards us... his face has turned quite scarlet, with the excitement and the heat... Suddenly he started screaming at the top of his voice: 'Now we'll show them! Anyone who stands in our way will be mown down. The German people have been soft for too long. Every Communist official must be shot. All friends of the Communists must be locked up. And that goes for the Social Democrats too...'

M From Goering's evidence to Judge Vogt at van der Lubbe's trial.

> People have wondered how it came about that my orders to arrest the ringleaders were carried out so promptly... on the night of the fire, I knew all the whereabouts of leading Communists because my predecessor had prepared a full list of their addresses and hideouts... that is why I was able to arrest thousands of Communists immediately after the fire.

N In a letter to *Der Spiegel*, 30 November 1959, H. Rauschning wrote:

> Goering did not describe these details to me..., but to a circle of friends, who surrounded him before we arrived. I heard no more than snatches of conversation... one of the group spotted me, he gave Goering a sign and Goering stopped talking... investigations have shown certain contradictions in my evidence... I admit, as a result I have grown less certain... Whether Goering was speaking the whole truth is quite a different matter. I never fully believed Goering's version.

O From *The Invisible Writing*, by A. Koestler, 1954. Koestler helped to prepare the Communist publicity for the mock trial against the Nazis in Paris in 1934.

> ...the complete inside story of the fire [the Communist version of Nazi guilt]... was based on isolated scraps of information, deduction, guesswork, and brazen bluff. The only certainty we had was that some Nazis had somehow contrived to burn down the building. Everything else was a shot in the dark.

P Report from Fireman Roth of the Berlin Fire Brigade.

> The glass of the 250 foot dome had burst in places so that flames could shoot through the cracks. The result was a considerable updraught which caused the air to be sucked through all the passages into the burning Chamber.

Q *Marinus van der Lubbe was tried and found guilty by the Nazis in Leipzig in 1933 of lighting the fires that destroyed the Reichstag. He was executed on 10 January 1934 despite world-wide appeals for mercy.*

Questions

1. Read Source **B**.
   a) Say in your own words what you think van der Lubbe hoped to achieve? 4
   b) Why was his statement not believed? 3
2. Read Sources **B**, **D**, **E** and **F** carefully. How convincing is the evidence there to show that the Nazis started the fire? Use precise references to the sources in your answer. 15
3. Read Sources **H–P** carefully. How strong is the evidence to show that the Nazis did not start the fire? Use precise references to the sources in your answer. 15
4. a) If, as Source **O** suggests, their information was doubtful, why were the Communists sure that the Nazis had started the fire? 3
   b) Examine Source **N** and compare it with Source **E**. How has Rauschning changed his view since 1933? 3
   c) Both Koestler and Rauschning have changed their evidence after a number of years. Why might each of them do this? Explain your answer carefully. 5
5. Study these two judgements made by historians:

   By instantly taking advantage of the fire to further their plans for dictatorship, the Nazis made the deed their own.

   J. Fest, *Hitler*, 1974.

   '... even if they [the Nazis] had nothing to do with the fire, ... this does not justify their subsequent illegalities and the reign of terror, they remain the evil men they always were. But the affair should change our estimate of Hitler's methods ... far from being the far sighted planner, he had a genius for improvisation ... he had no idea how he would transform his position into a dictatorship. The solution came to him amongst the smouldering ruins of the Reichstag that February evening. It was, in his own words, "a heaven-sent opportunity" ...'

   A. J. P. Taylor, *Who burnt the Reichstag*, 1960

   a) How do these two historians' judgements agree about the Nazis and the fire? 3
   b) Is the historian a better judge than the court? 9

Chapter 5 The Night of the Long Knives

A study in causation and motivation

A *Röhm and Hitler together, with SA troops in the background*

The Nazi party had two military organisations which were independent of the German army.

The SA had been formed by the Nazis in 1921 as a military organisation to protect their own meetings and to disrupt those of their opponents. It attracted many former soldiers to join who had no use for ordinary politics and wished to change things by more violent and revolutionary ways.

By 1930 it had become important to Hitler that the Nazis try to obtain power by legal means, through normal elections. The behaviour of the SA was now an embarrassment. To keep the SA in line Hitler appointed his old friend and Nazi, Ernst Röhm as leader in January 1931.

The SS began as a small and élite bodyguard for the Führer, commanded by Heinrich Himmler who was, himself, supposed to be supervised by Röhm. In terms of numbers the SS could not match the SA. In 1933 the SS numbered about 52 000 men compared to nearly 3 000 000 directly controlled by Röhm in the SA. The SA was more than ten times the size of the regular army.

On 30 June 1934 the SS was used to smash the SA in the events known as 'The Night of the Long Knives'. Röhm was killed and other members of the SA were rounded up by the SS and driven to a nearby prison. These men were later butchered by the SS. Hitler radioed the codeword 'Kolibri' (Hummingbird) to Berlin and the SS began the work of arresting the SA's leaders throughout Germany. They were taken and shot.

B From *Hitler speaks* by H. Rauschning, 1940. Hermann Rauschning was a minor Nazi offical who left the party in 1934 and went to America. Here he reports Röhm's words spoken during a drunken conversation in 1934.

Adolf's a swine ... He only associates with reactionaries now. His old friends aren't good enough for him. Adolf is turning into a gentleman. Adolf knows exactly what I want ... Not a second edition of the old Imperial Army. Are we revolutionaries or aren't we? The generals are a lot of old fogeys. Adolf is a civilian, an 'artist', an idler ... What he wants is to sit on the hill top and pretend he is God ...

C From *The Third Reich* by D. G. Williamson, 1982.

... only Ernst Röhm possessed a sufficiently strong power base to become an effective critic of, or, in the final resort, a challenge to Hitler ... Röhm continued to expand the SA until by the end of 1933 it was a potential army of some two and a half million men.

D An SA leader, commented about the SA in 1933:

> Everyone is arresting everyone else, avoiding the official channels, everyone is threatening everyone else with protective custody, everyone is threatening everyone else with Dachau [a concentration camp near Munich]. Businesses are being forced to dismiss any number of employees, and businesses are being compelled to take on employees without checking on their qualifications ... the best and most reliable officials have become uncertain about the hierarchy of authority; this clearly must have a destructive effect on the State. Every little street cleaner today feels he is responsible for matters which he has never understood.

E In a speech on 6 July 1933, Hitler said:

> Revolution is not a permanent state, it must be guided into the secure bed of evolution ... A businessman must not be dismissed if he is a good businessman; especially not if the National Socialist put in his place knows nothing about business ... we must not keep looking round to see what next to revolutionise ... History will judge us by whether we knew how to provide work ... The main thing now is the daily bread of five million people ... In the long run, the more successful the economic underpinning of our programme, the more secure will be our political power ... Reich Governors are responsible for seeing that no organisations or party authorities shall claim governmental rights, dismiss people or fill offices ...

F *The cartoonist, Flick, comments on SA tactics*

G *An 'auxilliary policeman' (SA member drafted into the police) standing guard over arrested Communists in 1933*

H General von Blomberg, Minister of Defence, 28 February 1934, said:

I refer again to the armed staff guards of the SA. Selection and training are being carried out with the intention of appearing in public. In terms of numbers this would amount to 6000–8000 men permanently armed ... in that military district alone ... Today I received a report that a staff guard armed like this is being formed in Hoechst am Main, that is to say, in the neutral zone ...

I Adapted from *Hitler's War Aims* By N. Rich, 1973.

Röhm advocated the incorporation of entire units of the SA into the regular army to convert it into a genuine people's army, or at any rate, a genuine Röhm army ...

J The Versailles Treaty, 1919 stated:

> *Clause 43*
> In the area defined [a 50 km corridor east of the Rhine] the assembly and maintenance of armed forces ... are ... forbidden.
>
> *Clause 160*
> ... the total number of the army must not exceed 100 000 men.

K From *A History of Modern Germany, 1840–1945* by H. Holborn, 1969.

The Army was not prepared to accept the SA leaders as officers. Röhm was angry. Noisy talk was heard in his camp demanding a second revolution to separate Hitler from his cooperation with the Generals ... it is possible that Röhm might have led a revolt against Hitler.

L From *Hitler: the man and the myth* by R. Manvell and H. Fraenkel, 1978.

> What Hitler had in mind was to take Hindenburg's place as absolute head of the state when the President died, inheriting with this position the army's allegiance. Since Hindenburg's death was, in the early months of 1934, expected at almost any time, Hitler had to prepare the army for so substantial a change as delicately as he might ...

M Adapted from *Hitler's War Aims* by N. Rich, 1973.

An alliance grew up between Goering and Himmler. ... Both men were inordinately ambitious, both saw in Röhm a major obstacle to their ambitions: Goering because he aspired to the control of Germany's armed forces; Himmler because as head of the SS, he resented his subordination to Röhm within the SA and Röhm's refusal to allow the SS to play a greater role in party and state affairs.

N Field-Marshall von Kleist, Army commander in Silesia, June 1934, recalled:

> I flew on 29 June to Berlin and reported ... 'I have the impression that we – Army and SA – are being egged on against each other by a third party ...' By that I meant Himmler ... much of the information came from him. General von Reichenau replied, 'That may be true, but it's too late now'.

[Reichenau was a very high ranking general and the right hand man of the Minister of Defence, General Blomberg.]

O From *A History of Modern Germany 1840–1945*, by H. Holborn, 1969.

There is no evidence to prove that he [Röhm] prepared a revolt in the Spring and Summer of 1934. For the time being at least, he apparently intended only to put pressure on Hitler.

The fact that nowhere was resistance shown and practically all were taken by surprise is another proof that the SA did not prepare a revolt.

P *They salute with both hands now. From the* London Evening Standard, *3 July 1934.*

Q Adapted from *The Black Corps* by R. Koehl, 1983.

The difficulty lay with the victory of January 1933 [Hitler's success in the elections] ... Hitler had only barely won power. The door had been opened to him because he was noisy and dangerous, but he had not captured the power as yet ... the powers of the German state, the army, the economy and the social institutions were immense ... Hitler, Goering, Goebbels, Hess, and Himmler ... discovered that to conquer a whole modern society requires time and technical ability ... a silent revolution in permanence ... for this the SS were best equipped. ... the ultimate crime of the SA was not radicalism and indiscipline but too much open ambition. Himmler and the SS leadership learned better to keep silent and to wait.

Questions
1. What caused Hitler to order the destruction of the SA in The Night of the Long Knives? 20
2. 'Secondary sources of evidence are likely to be more helpful in finding the causes of an event than primary sources.' Use the evidence in this chapter to decide whether you agree with this statement and to explain your answer. 10

Chapter 6 Propaganda

An exercise in understanding the reliability and usefulness of primary evidence

Between 1928 and 1933 the Nazi party enjoyed staggering success in national elections. In May 1928 they won 12 seats in the German Reichstag; two years later in September 1930, they had 107 members, by July 1932 their strength was 230. How can this dramatic success be explained?

Economic conditions at the time were important. Germany felt the effects of the depression more severely than other countries because of its close financial links with America. Groups of Germans with common interests such as farmers or businessmen tried to safeguard their financial position. They looked to political parties to help them. Therefore many small parties existed in the Reichstag representing the narrow aims of all these small groups. It became difficult with so many interest groups for the Reichstag to make decisions which satisfied everyone. Many people became disillusioned with the stagnation of Germany politics as everyone seemed only to be interested in looking after themselves. The Nazis used the situation to their advantage. They tried to appeal to people's personal grievances and at the same time to unite them in calls to support the German nation.

The idea of the German nation was very important to the Nazi view. They were successful in attracting votes and party members from amongst the young, the agricultural or Protestant areas, as well as from the middle class.

Apart from economic and political reasons, the Nazi party were so successful between 1928 and 1933 because of its excellent propaganda. As you study the following extracts, bear in mind the purpose of propaganda, its presentation and possible effects on people. Answer the questions that follow.

A *The massed ranks of 160 000 leaders of the Nazi party at Nuremberg at the end of the summer of 1933*

B *The Führer surrounded by a group of standard-bearers, during the Nuremberg Rally*

C From *Mein Kampf* by Adolf Hitler, 1925

The leader of genius must have the ability to make different opponents appear as if they belong to the one category ...

The memory of the masses is very restricted and their understanding is feeble ... they quickly forget. So all effective propaganda must be confined to a few bare essentials ... expressed in simple terms. These slogans should be persistently repeated ...

Propaganda must not investigate the truth ... (unless it) is favourable to its own side.

Men are won over less by than the written word than the spoken word ... every great movement owes its growth to great orators not writers.

The time of day at which the lecture takes place can have a decisive influence ... At night they give in more easily to the dominating force of a stronger will ...

The mass meeting is necessary because in it the individual, who ... feels alone ... for the first time gets the picture of a larger community ... he is swept away by three or four thousand others he has given in to the magic influence of what we call 'mass suggestion'.

D Orders issued to Nazi regional propaganda headquarters before the Presidential elections, April 1932.

> ... Hitler poster: The Hitler poster show a fascinating Hitler head on a completely black background. Subtitle: white on black 'Hitler'. In accordance with the Führer's wish this poster is to be put up only during the final days. Experience shows that during the final days [of the campaign] there is a variety of coloured posters, this poster will contrast with all the others and will produce a tremendous effect on the masses.
>
> Instructions for the National Socialist Press for the election:
> 1. From 29 March–10 April all papers must appear in an enlarged edition with a tripled circulation.
> 2. From 29 March–3 April a special topic must be dealt with every day on the front page of all our papers in a big spread: Hitler as a man; Hitler as a fighter (gigantic achievements through his will power, etc.); Hitler as a statesman – plenty of photos.
> 3. On 3 April, the great propaganda journey of the Führer through Germany will start, about a million people are to be reached directly through our Führer's speeches ...

E *A highly emotional crowd at a sports day in Breslau in 1938*

F Luis Solmitz, Hamburg school teacher, 1932, remembers:

The hours passed, the sun shone, expectations rose. Aeroplanes above us. Testing of the loudspeakers, buzzing of the cine-cameras. 'The Führer is coming!' A ripple went through the crowds. Around the speakers platform one could see hands raised in the Hitler salute. A speaker opened the meeting, abused the 'system', nobody listened to him. A second speaker welcomed Hitler and made way for the man who had drawn 120 000 people of all classes and ages. There stood Hitler in a simple black coat and looked over the crowd, waiting – a forest of swastika pennants swished up, the jubilation of this moment was given vent in a roaring salute. Main theme: Out of parties shall grow a nation, the German nation. His voice was hoarse after all his speaking during the previous days ... roaring enthusiasm and applause. How many look up to him with touching faith! as their helper, their saviour, their deliverer from unbearable distress.

G A Government description of Nazi Propaganda efforts, May 1930.

Carefully organised propaganda headquarters in each region make sure that the speaker and subject are adapted to the local and economic circumstances. Through courses, Nazi speakers are trained for this task over a period of months. They give at least thirty speeches over eight months and receive a fee of 20 Reichmarks per evening in addition to expenses. Halls are almost always overcrowded with enthusiastic listeners. Meetings with an audience of between 1000 and 5000 are a daily event in the bigger towns. Frequently such propaganda squads win the whole population for the movement through the most varied entertainment such as concerts, sports days, tattoos in suitable places and even church parades. National Socialist theatre groups travel from place to place.

H *An election campaign audience at a factory in Graz in 1938*

I Professor K. A. von Muller, who was present at a Nazi rally in 1923, recalls:

In the 'Lowenbrau' I heard him speak for the first time ... [I had never met] so hot a breath of hypnotic mass excitement. It was not only the special tension of these weeks, of this day. 'Their own battle songs, their flags, their own symbols, their own salute'. For hours, endless booming military music; for hours, short speeches by subordinate leaders. When was he coming? Nobody can describe the fever that spread in this atmosphere. Suddenly there was a movement at the back entrance. Words of command. The speaker on the platform stopped in mid-sentence. Everybody jumped up, saluting. And right through the shouting crowds and streaming flags the one they were waiting for came with his followers, walking quickly to the platform, high right arm raised stiffly. He passed by me quite close and I saw his thin, pale features contorted as if by inward rage, cold flames darting from his protruding eyes, which seemed to be searching out enemies to be conquered. Did the crowd give him this mysterious power? Did it come from him to them?

J From *I knew Hitler* by K. Ludecke, 1938, impressions of Hitler speaking in 1922.

My critical faculty was swept away ... I do not know how to describe the emotions that swept over me as I heard this man. When he spoke of the disgrace of Germany, I felt ready to spring on any enemy. His appeal to German manhood was like a call to arms; the gospel he preached, a sacred truth. I forgot everything but the man; the glancing around, I saw that his magnetism was holding these thousands as one. Of course I was ripe for this experience. I was a man of thirty-two, weary with disgust and disillusionment, a wanderer seeking a cause. The intense will of the man, the passion of his sincerity. I experienced a joy that could be likened only to religious conversion.

K *One of a series of photographs commissioned by Hitler from the photographer Heinrich Hoffman. This one shows Hitler practising an oratorical gesture*

L From *Hitler and I*, by Otto Strasser, 1940.

I have been asked many times what is the secret of Hitler's extraordinary power as a speaker. I can only attribute it to his uncanny intuition, which infallibly diagnoses the ills from which his audience is suffering. Adolf Hitler enters a hall. He snuffs the air. For a minute he gropes, feels his way, senses the atmosphere – suddenly he bursts forth. His words go like an arrow to their target he touches each private wound on the raw, liberating the mass unconscious, expressing its innermost aspirations, telling it what it most wants to hear.

M *The Führer receiving the adulation of an admirer in 1938*

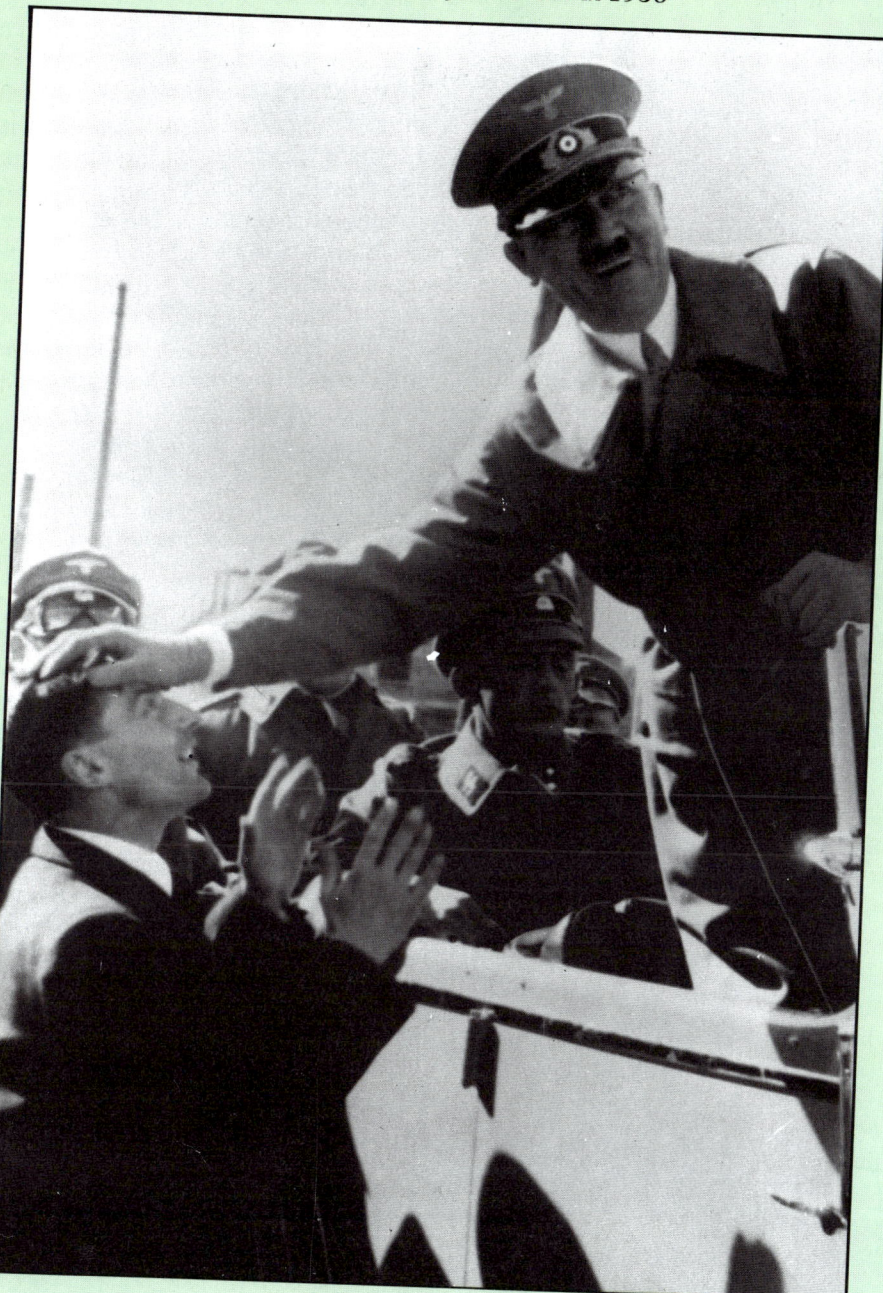

Questions

1. Read Sources **C**, **D** and **G**. Explain how Nazi propaganda tried to put Hitler's ideas about propaganda into practice. — 5
2. Look at the Sources **A**, **B**, **E**, **F**, **I**, **J** and **K**. Say which features of the way mass rallies were organised seem very important. You might mention:
    - Hitler's clothes and speech
    - the military aspects
    - the theatrical aspects
    - the atmosphere at Nazi meetings. — 15
3. The 'cult of the leader' was very important to the Nazi movement. Read Sources **F**, **I**, **K** and **L**, and look at Sources **E** and **M**.
    a) How far does this evidence help us to explain Hitler's popular leadership? — 10
    b) Did Hitler lead or follow his audience when speaking? — 5
4. Source **C** comes from Adolf Hitler's book, *Mein Kampf*, which explained his views on propaganda as early as 1925. Why, if his intentions and methods were well known, did his propaganda succeed? — 5
5. a) Are the visual sources more useful than the written sources for finding out about Nazi propaganda? Explain your answer with reference to each type of source. — 10
    b) In Source **J** the writer admits that his 'critical faculty was swept away'. Does this mean that we cannot rely upon his evidence? — 5
    c) The author of Source **I**, K. A. von Muller, was a historian as well as an eye witness. Do you think this makes his account more reliable? Give your reasons. — 5

Chapter 7 The Nazi police state

An exercise in the interpretation of primary evidence
[or an exercise in empathy]

The Nazis aimed to control all aspects of German life. One important way was through their domination of the courts, judges and legal system. The Nazis had increased the number of 'crimes' which carried the death penalty. Added to this were the various Nazi Police and security organisations like the Gestapo and SS. By 1936, the SS, led by Himmler, also controlled the ordinary German Police. The whole system gathered vast amounts of information about the lives and opinions of ordinary Germans. During the war period arrests were at the level of 15 000 per month. Some were 'political' prisoners such as Jews, gypsies, homosexuals and communists; others were charged with 'economic' crimes when they failed to work hard enough, complained about conditions or wanted more wages. In all, the Nazis arrested three million Germans. The SS, of course, had its own prison system in the concentration camps. Increasingly, from 1937, the SS interfered in the work of the courts, ignoring verdicts, putting those found innocent by the courts into concentration camps and intervening to have verdicts changed.

A *Heinrich Himmler, leader of the SS, during a parade in Munich in 1938. Behind him the SS officers Wolff, Heydrich and Heissmayer.*

B Hitler speaking in 1928:

> There is only one kind of law in this world and that lies in one's own strength.

C Hans Frick, Head of the Nazi Lawyers association, said in 1934:

> Everything which is useful for the nation is lawful; everything which harms it is unlawful.

D Extract from a law to change the Penal Code, 28 June 1935.

> National Socialism ... considers every attack on the welfare of the national community ... as wrong. In future therefore wrong may be committed in Germany even in cases where there is no law against what is being done. The law-maker cannot give exhaustive rules covering all the situations which may occur in life; he therefore entrusts the judge with filling in the remaining gaps ...

E The role of the Judge explained by the Nazi legal expert, Professor Karl Eckhardt, January 1936.

> The Judge ... is to safeguard the concrete order of the racial community, to prosecute all acts harmful to the community, and to arbitrate in disagreements. The National Socialist ideology especially as expressed in the party programme and in the speeches of our Führer, is the basis for interpreting legal sources.

F From *Justice in the Third Reich*, by I. Staff, 1964. An example of a trial in which the accused had signed a confession before coming to court. The events are described by the accused's lawyers.

> My client denied the crime. Then the Judge said: 'In that case we can begin with the hearing of the evidence. I intervened and asked permission to question the defendant, before hearing the evidence, about the circumstances in which he signed the statement ... and in particular whether he had been beaten by the officers of the Secret State Police in connection with the signing of these statements. The State Prosecutor jumped up and asked the president of the court to protect the officers of the Secret State Police against such attacks by the defence.
>
> The Appeal judge rose from his chair and said to me: 'Council for the defence, I must draw your attention to the fact ... that a question such as you have asked can lead to your being arrested in the courtroom and taken into custody. Do you wish to sustain the question?'
>
> ... into the dead silence came the words of the assistant judge, 'I will take it [the question] over on behalf of the court'. I got the impression that only a Judge who had been badly wounded in the 1914–18 war could get away with such courage. The cross-examination took about two hours. My client was released for lack of evidence.

G *Judge Freisher (centre) delivers the Nazi salute with a backdrop of the Nazi flag and a bust of Hitler*

H A case reported in Rhineland, July 1938.

> In a café a 64 year old woman remarked to her companion at the table: 'Mussolini has more political sense in one of his boots than Hitler has in his brain.' The remark was overheard and five minutes later the woman was arrested by the Gestapo who had been alerted by telephone.

I Decision of the State Labour Court, July 1934.

> By absenting himself from the premises before the start of the singing of the national anthem ... and by the failure to participate in parades ... an employee demonstrates his anti-State attitude. This justifies instant dismissal.

J *A cartoon by Gerstenberg showing the burning of books by the SS in 1933. Himmler looks on cheerfully*

K A Socialist opposed to the Nazis wrote this report in May 1937.

> The supervision is now so well organised ... Every staircase has an informer ... This 'staircase ruler' as one might call him, runs around with all sorts of forms and tries to find out about everything under the sun ... He is supposed to talk to the housewives about prices and food shortages, he pushes into people's homes, finds out what newspapers people read, what their lifestyle is like, etc.

L Socialist reports from around Germany.

> A large section of the population no longer reads a newspaper. basically the population is indifferent to what is in the papers ... the Nazis have persuaded the masses to leave politics to the men at the top ... Only really major events can rouse people.
> [North west Germany, June 1936]

> Of the vast majority of the population – looking at Communism –they declare; 'Well I'd rather have Hitler' ... Hitler is still outside the line of fire of criticism, whereas Goebbels is loathed even among the Nazis ... The reduction in unemployment, rearmament and the drive it shows in foreign policy are the big points in favour of Hitler's policy. [1936]

> The majority of people have two faces: one which they show to their good and reliable acquaintances; and the other for the authorities, the party offices, keen Nazis, and for strangers. The private face shows criticism ... the official one beams optimism and contentment.
> [South Germany, 1937]

> The most shocking thing is the ignorance about what is actually going on in Germany ... They are completely convinced there are no longer concentration camps ... They simply do not want to believe that the Nazis treat their opponents with ruthless brutality ... it would be too terrible for them, they prefer to shut their eyes to it. Even in the case of arrests of opponents of the regime only a few families hear about it and even the neighbourhood remains completely in the dark.
> [North Germany, 1938]

M *SS troops salute Hitler*

Questions
1. Use Sources **B–D** to explain the Nazis' attitude to the Law.   7
2. Use Sources **D–F** to explain what is the judge's role in the legal process? You should use the sources to illustrate your answer.   7
3. Using Sources **H–L** say what effects you think a police state had upon its citizens and why these effects would have come about.   16

Empathy Question. How do you think that the German people would have reacted to information about the concentration camps?   30

You may be better able to answer this question after studying Chapter 6 and 8.

Chapter 8 Holocaust

An exercise in the use and evaluation of diaries, autobiography and fiction, as historical evidence

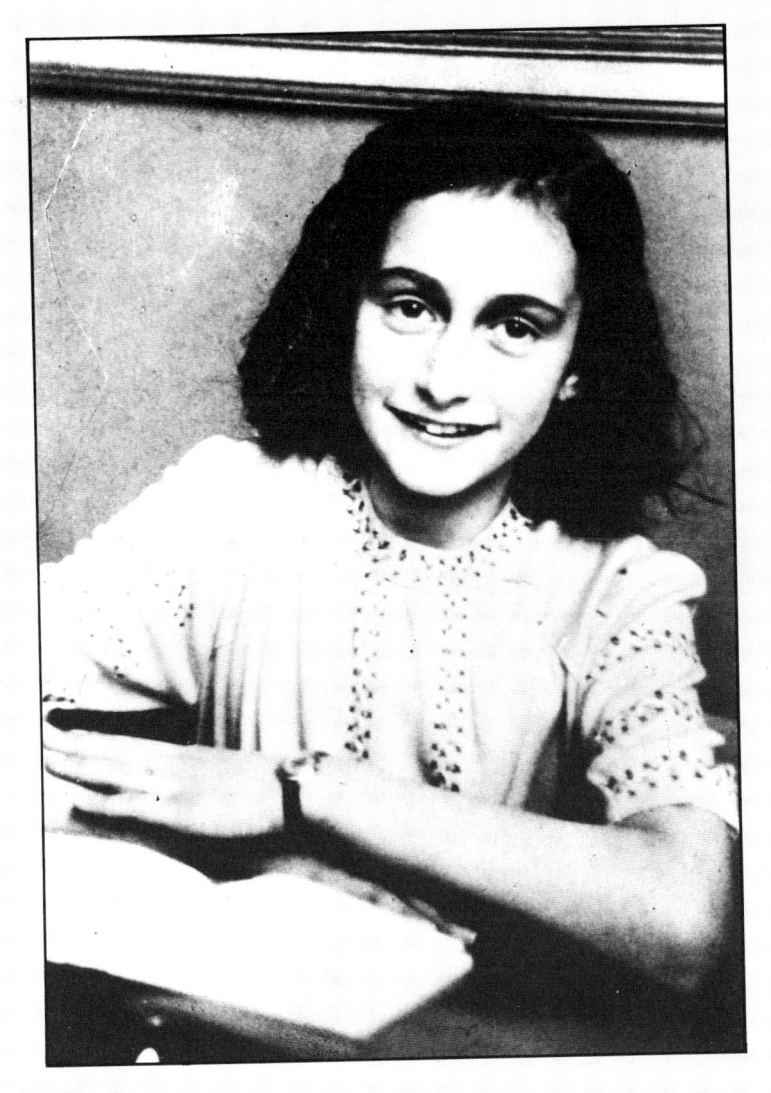

As the Nazis gained control of more of Europe, Jews and other groups whom Hitler despised suffered cruelty and death. From 1939, Hitler and the Nazis increased the scale and intensity of their campaign to destroy those believed to be 'inferior'.

The Nazis created ghettos in large cities in Eastern Europe to contain the Jews while they waited to be sent to concentration camps. Those who managed to stay alive in the ghettos were gradually reduced in number as train-loads of them were transported to the death camps. In the camps like Auschwitz, Treblinka and Dachau, Jews were killed by gassing, forced labour, experimentation, shooting, malnutrition and disease. It is thought that as many as six million people died. Many more suffered but survived.

The pictures tell the story of how the Nazis treated the Jews. After you have looked at them read the three sources.

A *Anne Frank. Anne Frank was a Jewish girl who was 13 in 1942, when she, her parents and sister went into hiding from the Germans in the sealed-off back rooms of an office building in Amsterdam. In 1944 they were betrayed to the Gestapo and taken to concentration camps. With the exception of Anne's father, they all died. The diary which Anne kept during those two years was later found and published in 1947.*

B From Anne Frank's diary, Saturday, 20 June 1942.

> I don't intend to show this diary to anyone, unless I find a real friend ... the reason for starting my diary ... is that I have no such real friend ... I want this diary itself to be my friend, and I shall call my friend Kitty ... After May 1940, good times rapidly fled: first the war, then capitulation, followed by the arrival of the Germans. That is when the sufferings of us Jews really began. Anti-Jewish decrees followed each other in quick succession. Jews must wear a yellow star, Jews must hand in their bicycles, Jews are banned from trams and are forbidden to drive. Jews are only allowed to do their shopping between three and five o'clock and then only in shops which bear the placard 'Jewish shop'. Jews must be indoors by eight o'clock and cannot even sit in their own gardens after that hour. Jews are forbidden to visit the theatres, cinemas and other places of entertainment. Jews may not take part in public sports. Swimming-baths, tennis courts, hockey fields and other sports grounds are all prohibited to them. Jews may not visit Christians. Jews must go to Jewish schools ...

C From Anne Frank's diary, Friday, 9 October 1942.

Dear Kitty,
I've only got dismal and depressing news for you today. Our many Jewish friends are being taken away by the dozen. These people are being treated by the Gestapo without a shred of decency, being loaded into cattle trucks and sent to Westerbork, the big Jewish camp in Drente. Westerbork sounds terrible: only one washing cubicle for a hundred people and not nearly enough lavatories. There is no separate accommodation. Men, women, and children all sleep together ... It is impossible to escape; most of the people in the camp are branded as inmates by their shaven heads and many also by their Jewish appearance.
If it is as bad as this in Holland whatever will it be like in the distant and barbarous regions they are sent to? ... The British radio speaks of them being gassed. Perhaps that is the quickest way to die. I feel terribly upset ...

D From Anne Frank's diary, Thursday, 19 November 1942.

Dear Kitty,
Dussel has told us a lot about the outside world, which we have missed for so long now. He had very sad news. Countless friends and acquaintances have gone to a terrible fate. Evening after evening the green and grey army lorries trundle past. The Germans ring at every front door to enquire if there are any Jews living in the house. If there are, then the whole family has to go at once ... Sometimes they let them off for cash – so much per head. It seems like the slave hunts of olden times. In the evenings when it is dark, I often see rows of good, innocent people accompanied by crying children, walking on and on, in charge of a couple of these chaps, bullied and knocked about until they almost drop. No one is spared – old people, babies, expectant mothers, the sick – each and all join in the march of death ... All because they are Jews.

E *A ghetto wall being constructed*

F From *For those I have loved* by Martin Gray, 1971. Martin Gray is a Jew and grew up in Warsaw, Poland, during the war. As a youth he smuggled food into the ghetto part of Warsaw in which he lived. In the summer of 1942, when the Nazis increased their efforts to destroy the Jews, Martin Gray was captured and sent to the concentration camp of Treblinka. Fortune saved him from immediate gassing. He worked in the camp and eventually escaped. He joined the Polish Resistance movement and then fought with the Russian army as they pushed the German army back to Berlin from the east.

I found out that they were building a brick wall ... the whole street was to be sealed off: we'd be penned in like beasts. ...

I was walking in Nalewki Street, dreaming away, when the trucks stopped and I had to go down on all fours like all the rest, I'd have to jump like a frog, and do it well, but even that wouldn't prevent my getting struck on the back, the soldiers would laugh and belt me ... the whole street were on all fours and the soldiers were firing head-high.

A few yards ahead of me a woman ... in the middle of the road, was resisting, trying to hold onto a baby, and two huge soldiers were wresting it from her. I could see her staring eyes ... panic-stricken ... They grabbed the child, playing catch with it; there she was, holding out her arms, not knowing who to approach, trying to seize the child which wasn't even crying. Then one of the soldiers dropped it. The trucks moved off again ... All anyone could talk about was the massacre which had taken place in the streets of Warsaw. Hundreds of Jews had been killed, others had been taken away to the forest.

G *Jews led away at gunpoint after an uprising in the Warsaw Ghetto in 1943*

H From *For those I have loved* by Martin Gray, 1971.

I was still alive. The stench in the hut was intolerable. Men were groaning, others prayed. I was sitting next to a man who was trembling, his eyes fixed his fists and jaws clenched. He was wearing a red badge: a veteran of the camp. 'Where do they go, the rest from the train?'. 'The gas chambers'. 'Where?'. 'To the lower camp'. I huddled against the wooden wall. My people, thousands of them, Warsaw! Men were crying in the darkness. Then the sound of a box overturning and a death rattle. Someone began praying. A suicide. I made up my mind ... not to settle for a cowardly death. They were taking our lives; it meant that our lives were jewels. My people were dead; I held their lives in trust. Through me vengeance would live on. I'd decided to live. I *would* escape – for those I loved. In the morning four bodies were dangling from the beams ...

By the second day I found out about life and death in Treblinka ... I saw prisoners killed with shovels. I saw dogs attack inmates. I knew why you had to walk with your head down, why you always had to run, do better, go faster: because the SS and the Ukrainians killed us to spur us on. There wasn't any shortage of us. Death reaped our ranks constantly. Slowing down at work: death. Carrying too light a load: death. Chewing a bit of food: death.

They created another kind of time at Treblinka ... marked by the arrival of the trains ... I carried clothes to the sorting lot ... helped the men to undress. I carried sackfuls of women's hair from the huts, where the women first undressed and were then shorn with a few snips. I made piles; all the objects were sorted, classified. Poor Jews from Warsaw, from the ends of Europe, crockery, fountain pens, photos of children. each object was a sorrow; a life with its maze of joys and hopes, a dead life.

I *Prisoners on a train destined for Auschwitz*

J From *Those I loved* by Martin Gray, 1972.

... We walked round the brick building. The guards raised their whips and clubs, and I too began to rush to the stretchers which they were indicating. We ran towards the broad open doors on the side of the building. ... Then we saw. For this I need still another voice, other words. The bodies were naked, entwined ... the bodies were yellow and blood had dribbled down their faces from their noses. We copied the others grabbed the bodies and ran. We paused in front of prisoners who, armed with pliers, were searching the corpses mouths and extracting the gold teeth, and ran over to the grave dug in the yellow sand. At the bottom, prisoners standing on the dead were lining up the bodies. We threw in our first body. I had become one of the *Totenjuden*, death-Jews.

Here were the depths. The depths of life. They'd invented this murder factory ... so well planned with nozzles, white-tiled walls, narrow entrance doors, sloping floor which ran down to the large door ...

K Inmates of a concentration camp. No notice is taken of the dead man on the floor in the background.

L From *Those I have loved* by Martin Gray, 1972.

Many of the prisoners seemed to live as if they did not know what they were doing, as if their actions had lost all meaning ... shadows of men carrying out given tasks, amid blows and in fear.

Sometime we found living children among the warm bodies ... little children, still alive, clinging to their mother's bodies. We strangled them with our own hands before throwing them into the grave. And we risked our lives doing it because we were wasting time. When we had completed our task we had to wait for the next wave. We heard it coming. We listened to the frenzied yells, the dogs barking. Sometimes we found men multilated, their stomachs torn open by the dogs. Dogs trained by men.

I need another voice, other words to describe the shame that filled me, nausea, shame at still being alive; and the compulsion to live that possessed me; to live, to tell what we'd seen, what they'd done, What they'd forced us to do.

M *Inmates in Auschwitz had to load the bodies of their fellow-prisoners into ovens for cremation*

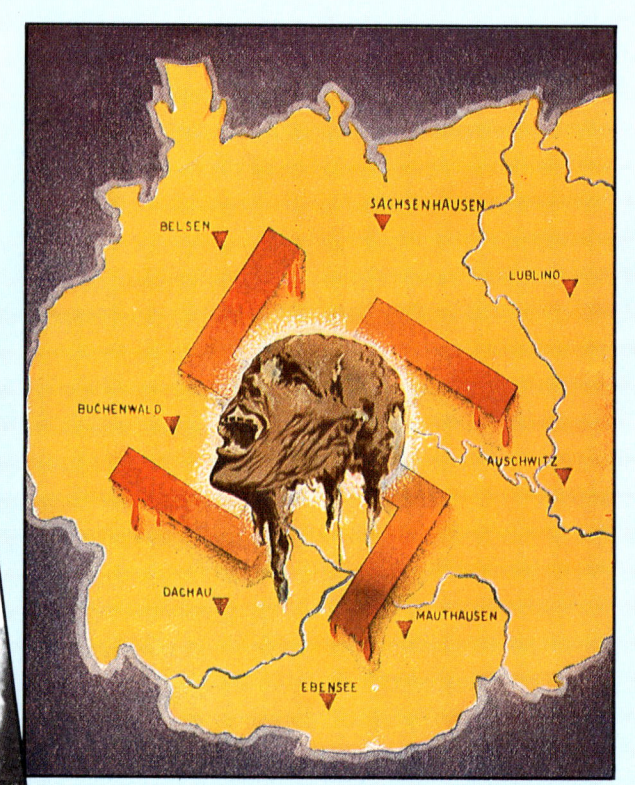

N *Locations of concentration camps*

40

O From *The Odessa File*, by Frederick Forsyth, 1972. These extracts are part of Frederick Forsyth's best-selling novel. In the story, this document was found amongst the possessions of an old, poor Jew who had committed suicide and it recounts some of his experiences in the Jewish ghetto of Riga during the war.

My name is Salomon Tauber, I am a Jew ... When I came out of the concentration camps of Riga and Stuthof, when I survived the Death March to Magdeburg, when the British soldiers liberated my body there in April 1945, leaving my soul in chains, I hated the world ... But with the passing of the years I have learned again to love ... one can forgive even what they did. But one can never forget.

... There were a few German SS officers standing in the shade of the station awning, distinguishable only when my eyes were accustomed to the light. One stood aloof on a packing crate, surveying the several human skeletons who emptied themselves from the train with a thin but satisfied smile – The Butcher of Riga – It was my first sight of SS-Captain Eduard Roschmann.

... Work was begun to expand or begin the six extermination camps of Auschwitz, Treblinka, Belzec, Sobibor, Chelmno and Maidanek. Until they were ready, however a place had to be found to exterminate as many as possible and 'store' the rest. Riga was chosen. Between August 1941 and October 14 1944, almost 200 000 exclusively German and Austrian Jews were shipped to Riga. Eighty thousand stayed there dead, 120 000 were shipped on to the six extermination camps and 400 came out alive ...

... the conditions in the ghetto grew worse. Each morning the entire population, mainly men, for women and children were exterminated on arrival in far greater percentages than the work-fit males, was assembled ... almost the whole population left the ghetto each day to work twelve hours at forced labour in the growing host of workshops nearby.

Our food rations were a half-litre of so-called soup, mainly tinted water, sometimes with a knob of potato in it ... in the mornings, and another half-litre, with a slice of black bread and a mouldy potato on return to the ghetto at night. Bringing food into the ghetto was punishable by immediate hanging before the assembled population at evening roll-call ... The males among them would mount the gallows platform and wait with the rope around their neck while the roll-call was completed. Then Roschmann would walk along the line, grinning up at the faces above him and kicking the chairs out from under, one by one. He liked to do this from the front, so the person about to die would see him. Sometimes he would pretend to kick the chair away, only to pull his foot back in time.

When a woman was caught bringing food into the camp she was made to watch the hangings of the men first, especially if one was her husband or brother. Then Roschmann made her kneel in front of the rest of us, while the camp barber shaved her bald. After roll-call she would be taken to the cemetry outside the wire, made to dig a shallow grave, then kneel beside it while Rochman or one of the others fired a bullet from his Lüger point-blank into the base of the skull ... he would often fire past the ear of the woman to make her fall into the grave with shock, then climb out again and kneel in the same position. Other times he would fire on an empty chamber, so there was just a click when the woman thought she was about to die.

... By the end of that first winter I was certain I could not survive much longer. The hunger, the cold, the damp, the overwork and the constant brutalities had whittled my formerly strong frame down to a mass of skin and bones ... I was just turned thirty-five and looked double that. I had witnessed the departure of tens of thousands to the forest of the mass graves, the deaths of hundreds from cold, exposure and overwork, and of scores from hanging, shooting, flogging and clubbing.

I should here describe the method of execution of those unfit for labour, for in this manner between 70 000 and 80 000 Jews were exterminated under the orders of Eduard Roschmann at Riga ... these victims were marched in a column to a forest outside the town ... in clearings between the pines enormous ditches had been dug by the Riga Jews before they died ... here the Latvian SS guards mowed them down so that they fell into the ditches. The remaining Riga Jews then filled in enough earth to cover the bodies, adding one more layer of corpses to those underneath until the ditch was full. Then a new one was started. From the ghetto we could hear the clattering of the machine guns when each new consignment was liquidated ... lorries full of clothes were brought to the Tin Square for sorting. They made a mound as big as a house until they were sorted out into piles of shoes, socks, underpants, trousers, dresses, jackets, shaving brushes, spectacles, dentures, wedding rings ... this was standard procedure ... all those killed were stripped at the graveside ... The gold, silver and jewellery was taken in charge by Roschmann personally ...

P *Dead inmates at Nordhausen surveyed by American forces*

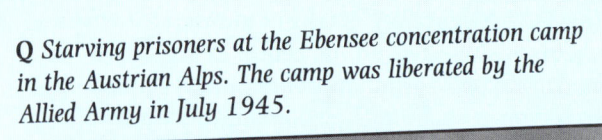

Q *Starving prisoners at the Ebensee concentration camp in the Austrian Alps. The camp was liberated by the Allied Army in July 1945.*

Questions

1. What are the limitations of Sources **B**, **C** and **D** as historical documents? **3**
2. How does the purpose of Anne Frank, Martin Gray and Frederick Forsyth differ? Explain your answer with precise reference to each of the sources **9**
3. a) How does the author of Source **O** try to persuade the reader that the document is real and true? **3**
   b) Does Source **O** have any value to someone studying the Holocaust? **3**
4. What difficulties does the historian have in writing about the Nazis' treatment of the Jews? **3**
5. 'Photographs arouse but don't express emotions.' Explain whether you think that the visual sources are better than the written sources for understanding what happened to the Jews? **9**

Chapter 9 The Hitler Youth

A study of a movement and its influence

A leading Nazi teacher said, 'Those who have youth on their side control the future'. The Nazis placed great importance on organising and controlling young people. For this purpose they created the Nazi Youth movements, there were groups for boys and girls of different ages. Pressure was put on young people to join them.

Not only was their leisure time organised, but also school time was used to influence the young. For this the Nazis needed to control the teachers. The teachers were organised by the Nazis through the National Socialist Teachers League. A combination of intimidation and propaganda increased membership to 97 per cent of all teachers in Germany by 1937. The Nazi Teachers League controlled promotions in the schools and continued indoctrinating teachers. However, many teachers became disillusioned because they had joined in the hope of improving the schools and this did not happen. Others were put off by the crudity of Nazi propaganda.

A *A fund-raising poster for the Youth movement*

B Adolf Hitler said, in a speech December 1938:

> What we look for from our German youth is different from what people wanted in the past. In our eyes the German youth of the future must be slim and slender, swift as the greyhound, tough as leather, and hard as Krupp steel.

C *Colour-in and cut-out figures from a German children's book, 1932*

D *Excited children and adults salute Hitler as he passes in a train*

E *Propaganda photograph of German school children*

F Nazi Youth law, 1 December 1936.

> The future of the German nation depends upon its youth and must be prepared for its future duties... The whole of German youth is organised in the Hitler Youth. All German young people, apart from being educated at home and at school, will be educated in the Hitler Youth physically, intellectually, and morally in the spirit of National Socialism to serve the nation and the community.

G Nazi law, 25 March 1939.

> All young people are required from the age of 10 to their nineteenth birthday to serve in the Hitler Youth.

H Hitler Youth Membership for 1932–1939 (number of people)

Year	Total membership	Total population (aged 10–18 years)
1932	107 956	
1933	2 292 041	7 529 000
1934	3 577 565	7 682 000
1935	3 943 303	8 172 000
1936	5 437 601	8 656 000
1937	5 879 955	9 060 000
1938	7 031 226	9 109 000
1939	7 287 470	8 870 000

I From *Youth in the Third Reich* by A. Klönne, 1982.

What I liked about the HJ [Hitlerjugend, i.e. Hitler Youth] was the comradeship. I was full of enthusiasm ... what boy isn't fired by high ideals such as comradeship, loyalty, and honour ... the trips ... off into the countryside ... made a fire ... have a sing song and tell stories ... I was pleased that sport had its place ... We never went on our trips without a ball or some piece of sports equipment.

Later when I became a leader the negative aspects became obvious. I found the compulsion and the requirement of absolute obedience unpleasant. It was preferred that people should not have a will of their own ... the HJ was interfering everywhere in people's private lives.

In our troop the activities consisted of almost entirely of stolid military drill. Even if sport or shooting practice or a sing song was scheduled, we always had to do drill first ... Why didn't we complain to parents and teachers? The only explanation I can find is that we were all in the grip of ambition; we wanted to impress our sub-leaders with exemplary discipline, our powers of endurance, with our military bearing.

J *A troop of girls from the Hitler Youth*

K From *Account Rendered* by M. Maschmann, 1964.

... the Hitler Youth allowed themselves to be dressed in uniforms and regimented ... their characteristic surplus of energy and thirst for action found great scope in their programme of activities.

... It was part of the method of the National Socialist Youth leadership to arrange almost everything in the form of competitions. It was not only in sport and one's profession that one competed. Every unit wanted to have the best group 'home', the most interesting expedition log, the biggest collection for the Winter Relief Fund ... In the musical competitions Hitler Youth choirs, fife and drum bands, chamber orchestras and amateur theatrical groups competed ... even story telling competitions. This constant competition introduced an element of unrest and forced activity into the life of the groups.

L *Young members of the the Hitler Youth movement in 1933*

M From an SPD report, 1934.

> Youth is still in favour of the system: the novelty, the drill, the uniform, the camp life, the fact that school and the parental home take a back seat compared to the community of young people – all that is marvellous. A great time without any danger ... The new generation has never had much use for education ... on the contrary, knowledge is publicly condemned ... the parents cannot forbid the child to do what all children are doing, cannot refuse him the uniform ... the young people follow the instructions of the HJ and demand from their parents that they become good Nazis, that they give up Marxism, Reaction, and dealings with Jews ... Old men make no impression nowadays ... the secret of National Socialism is the secret of its youth. The chaps are so fanaticized that they believe in nothing but their Hitler.

N *A propaganda poster for the Hitler Youth*

O *A Hitler Youth orchestra*

P *Anti-Jewish propaganda from a German children's book, 1938*

Q An official of The National Socialist Teachers' League, 1937, said:

German youth must no longer be confronted with choice ... it must be consciously shaped according to the principles of National Socialism.

R From German Institute of Education guidelines for the teaching of History, 1938.

The German nation in its essence and greatness is the subject of the teaching of history ... educating young people to respect the great German past and to have faith in the mission and future of their own nation ... the clear recognition of the basic racial forces of the German nation ... history must not appear as a chronicle which strings events together indiscriminately. Only the important events should be portrayed in history lessons ... it must always show greatness ... the powerless and insignificant have no history.

S Tests from German Mathematics text books.

Question 95 The construction of a lunatic asylum cost 6 million RM. How many houses at 15 000 RM each could have been built for that amount?

Question 97 (b) A modern night bomber can carry 1 800 incendiaries. How long (km) is the path along which it can distribute these bombs if it drops a bomb every second at a speed of 250 kmph?

T From 'Young people: For or Against the Nazis', by D. Peukert, in *History Today*, October 1985.

Those whose adolescence fell in the years 1933–1936 had already had important experiences before the Nazi seizure of power ... Young people of 1936–1939 had no such memories. They had gone through schools that bore the stamp of National Socialism ... the Hitler Youth was something taken for granted ... there was no alternative ... a rival to the traditional authorities of home and school. Involvement in its activites offered simultaneously the promise of making a name for oneself but also uniformity. This feature grew stronger as the Hitler Youth became more bureaucratic ... its leadership grew older ... the use of coercion increased. The group whose adolescence occurred during the war years 1939–1945 experienced the empty aspects of daily life in the Hitler Youth.

In practice, contradictions arose ... military conscription robbed the Hitler Youth of many badly needed older Youth leaders. Competition between the school and the Hitler Youth gave rise to conflict in which young people could play one off against the other. National Socialism remained much too vague.

No one in our class read *Mein Kampf*. I myself only took quotations from the book ... we didn't know much about Nazi ideology ... anti-semitism was brought in rather marginally at school for example via Richard Wagner's essay 'The Jews in music'. Nevertheless we were politically programmed: to obey orders, standing to attention and saying 'Yes, Sir.' and to stop thinking when the magic word 'Fatherland' was uttered ...

U From 'Young people: For or Against the Nazis' by D. Peukert in *History Today*, October 1985.

With the Hitler Youth as a large scale bureaucratic organisation ... the ageing of its leadership in the course of the 1930s, the attraction to young people began to decline. The campaign to bring everyone into the HJ ranks brought in those who had previously proclaimed their antipathy [dislike] simply by their absence. Disciplinary and surveillance measures made harmless and everyday pleasures, such as meetings of friends, criminal offences. Above all the claim of legal powers by Hitler Youth patrols whose members were scarcely older than the young people they were keeping track of, provoked general indignation.

The belief that the Hitler Youth successfully mobilised young people is only half the story. By the end of the 1930s thousands of young people were turning away from the leisure activities of the Hitler Youth.

V From 'Young people: For or Against the Nazis' by D. Peukert in *History Today*, October 1985.

For many young people in the provinces the arrival of the Hitler Youth meant the first access to leisure activities in a youth organisation ... the openings for girls was even greater. Girls could escape from the female role-model centred around the family and children ... pursue activities otherwise reserved for boys.

Questions

1. Refer to Sources **B** and **F**. Why were young people considered to be important to the Nazis? — 3
2. How did the Nazis try to win the 'hearts and minds' of young people? You might consider the attractions of the Hitler Youth, its rewards and punishments. — 8
3. Refer to Sources **I**, **M** and **T**. Why were many people frightened by the activities of the Hitler Youth? — 3
4. What do the pictures and Sources **R** and **S** show about the nature of the Nazi education? — 2
5. Refer to Sources **F**, **G**, **H** and **I**. Why did it become necessary to make laws about joining the Hitler Youth? — 6
6. How much impact did the Hitler Youth have on the young people of Germany? — 8

Chapter 10 The German economy under the Nazis

An exercise in the interpretation and analysis of evidence

In order to improve Germany's economic strength Hitler began a four year plan, with industrial targets for 1936. However he had to balance the need to make Germany more powerful with the need to provide the things for ordinary people to buy.

A Hitler said in 1936:

> Our military development cannot be too large, nor its pace too swift ... If we do not succeed in bringing the German army as rapidly as possible to be the premier army in the world ... then Germany will be lost! ... all other desires without exception must come second to this task ... When our nation has six or seven million unemployed, the food situation improves because these people lack purchasing power ... but the effect of undernourishment must gradually be deducted from the body of our nation ... Thus despite the difficult food situation, the most important task of our economic policy is to see to it that all Germans are incorporated into the economic process ... The final solution lies in extending our living space ... the sources of raw materials and food of our people.
>
> I consider it necessary that now with iron determination, a 100 per cent self-sufficiency should be achieved in every area possible ... and that the nation in most essential raw materials be made independent of other countries we should thus save the foreign currency which in peacetime we need for our import of foodstuffs. Only [then] will it be possible for the first time to demand sacrifices from the German people in the economy and in food.

B Military expenditure: Germany, Britain and USA, 1933–1945 as a percentage of Gross National Product.

Year	Germany	USA	Britain
1933	3	1	3
1934	6	1	3
1935	8	1	2
1936	13	1	5
1937	13	1	7
1938	17	1	8
1939	23	1	22
1940	38	2	53
1941	47	11	60
1942	55	31	64
1943	61	42	63
1944	?	42	62
1945	?	36	53

C Public spending on work creation projects in Germany in millions of Reichmarks.

Purpose	Public spending (millions of Reichmarks)	
	Year ending 1933	Year ending 1934
Public building	855.6	1002.4
Housing	723.3	1280
Transport	950.8	1683.9
[autobahn total]	[50]	[350]
Agriculture	337.4	389.2
Other measures	70	70
Labour exchanges + Welfare offices	164	568
Total	3101.1	4993.5
Arms spending	1900	5900

D *Hitler initiates the construction of the first autobahn (from Frankfurt to Darmstadt) in 1934*

E The Nazi drive towards self-sufficency in important commodities (thousand of tons)

Commodity	Output			Plan target
	1936	1938	1942	1940
Oils and petrol	1 790	2 340	6 260	13 830
Aluminium	98	166	260	273
Buna rubber	0.7	5	96	120
Explosives	18	45	300	223
Steel	19 216	22 656	20 480	24 000
Coal	319 782	381 171	411 977	453 500

F *Hitler at the Volkswagen factory at Fallersleben near Wolfsburg. Porsche is in the raincoat. 25 June 1938*

I *Professor Ferdinand Porsche, one of the innovators in the German vehicle industry*

J A Socialist reports of how the Nazis reduced unemployment, 1934:

The assignment of armaments contracts. The extension of short time work through pressure on employers to avoid redundancies and take on new workers even when not needed. Wage cuts. Work creation projects of doubtful economic value. Deporting young unemployed workers to the countryside as farm labourers. The ruthless weeding out of those who receive welfare benefits.

... South Bavaria ... people are exhausted by heavy road works. They are mostly long-term unemployed lacking in strength because of poor nutrition. They must carry out heavy gravel work, if possible without machinery. ...

... Baden ... At the Autobahn construction site near Mannheim there is a terrible system of slave-driving: fear produces an unheard-of work tempo ... overseers standing on mounds and watching ... shouting at the workers one is reminded of descriptions of Ancient Rome.

G German self-sufficiency in important foods (percentages)

Food	1927/8	1933/4	1938/9
Bread	79	99	115
Potatoes	96	100	100
Vegetables	84	90	91
Sugar	100	99	101
Meat	91	98	97
Eggs	64	80	82
Fats	44	53	57

H German unemployment

Year	January	July
1932	6 042 000	5 392 000
1933	6 014 000	4 464 000
1934	3 773 000	2 426 000
1935	2 974 000	1 754 000
1936	2 520 000	1 170 000
1937	1 853 000	563 000
1938	1 052 000	218 000
1939	302 000	38 000

K Hooray, the butter is finished! Goering in his Hamburg speech: 'Ore has always made an empire strong, butter and lard have only served to make its people fat.'

Hurrah, die Butter ist alle!
Goering in seiner Hamburger Rede: „Erz hat stets ein Reich stark gemacht, Butter und Schmalz haben höchstens ein Volk fett gemacht"

L A Socialist opposed to the Nazis stated in 1938:

The Nazis try to persuade the people ... the blame lies in Germany's one-sided dependence on foreign countries, which shows in a shortage of foreign currency ... in reality it is because of the overloading of Germany's economic strength through rearmament and the self-sufficiency programme.

Under the lash of dictatorship, economic activity has greatly increased. The exploitation of labour has greatly increased by the abolition of the 8 hour day, increase in the work rate, more female employment. The most important method of 'diverting' production from consumer goods to rearmament is in pinching the consumers' purse as hard as possible ... by keeping down wages and raising taxes.

As long as the German people are prepared to put up with their living standards being held at the lowest of levels ... each year 12–13 billion Reichmarks are squeezed from the national income for rearmament. But even then one cannot do everything at once ... increase land and air forces, build up a massive battle fleet, fortify new extended borders ... On the living standards of the German people so far, one can either do one or the other or a bit of everything, but not everything at the same time and in unlimited dimensions.

Questions
1. Explain Hitler's economic priorities as stated in Source **A**? — 5
2. Refer to Sources **B, C, E, G,** and **H**. To what extent do the figures show that these priorities have been achieved successfully? — 9
3. What according to the authors of Sources **J** and **L** are the failings of Hitler's economic policies? — 6
4. In this chapter there is documentary, statistical and photographic evidence. What are the advantages of each type of source for determining the success of Hitler's economic policies? Refer to specific sources in your answer. — 10

Chapter 11 Opposition and appeasement: 1938

A study in the analysis of historical narrative

The following extract has been adapted from *The History of the German Resistance, 1933–1945* by Peter Hoffman, 1970.

In 1936 Hitler reoccupied the area along the River Rhine. This Rhineland area had been forbidden to German troops under the Versailles Treaty which ended the First World War. Britain and France did not take any action; Britain said that it was really German territory anyway. In March 1938 Hitler took over Austria, in what was termed the 'Anschluss' or union of Austria and Germany. This was accomplished by Hitler's armies without any fighting. Most Austrians were German speaking and had strong cultural ties with Germany. Chamberlain, the British Prime Minister, said in Parliament, 'The hard fact is that nothing could have arrested what actually has happened – unless this country and other countries had been prepared to use force'. With this success Hitler turned to his next target, the part of Czechoslovakia known as the Sudentenland.

Despite Hitler's success in Germany, there were some important Germans who did not agree with his ideas. The reason they opposed Hitler was because they wanted to keep the peace in Europe, and Hitler's policies seemed to be leading towards war. Many of these Germans worked within the Nazi party to try to bring about change in their government's policy. One of them was Dr Carl Goerdeler. He worked in a senior economic post for the Nazis until 1937. After his resignation he was funded by some German businessmen to visit other

A *German troops parade through Vienna after the 'Anschluss' in 1938*

countries' governments to point out how dangerous Hitler was. Both the British and French governments listened to Goerdeler as a spokesman for the German opposition. His view was that Hitler should be given the part of Czechoslovakia that he claimed, *but* that a strong line be drawn and there should be no further concessions given.

Very few people in Britain realised how war-like Hitler's plans were. The British official who had spoken to Geordeler in 1937 wrote a report for the new Prime Minister, Neville Chamberlain, urging a hard-line approach towards Hitler. The report said that Germany was militarily weak and that many high-ranking people close to Hitler wanted peace. Because of this, those who opposed Hitler deserved support from outside. However, some British politicians and officials thought that the opposition to Hitler only wanted to remove him so that they could take power themselves. Why help to overthrow Hitler only to have to grant concessions to the new government? It was also pointed out that what Goerdeler was proposing was treason. Possibly for these reasons, Britain's Foreign Secretary, Anthony Eden, decided that the report should not be passed on. Chamberlain had already decided on a policy of compromise with regard to Austria and Czechoslovakia; the British Generals told him that the British army was in no way ready for war with Germany.

Early in April 1938 there was another contact with the German opposition. An important landowner, Ewald von Kleist contacted the British government indirectly warning of Hitler's plans for conquest. He said that Czechoslovakia would be next and only a firm NO would stop Hitler. Through the same contact, three German generals informed the British government that Czechoslovakia would be seized on 28 September. They thought that some resistance to Hitler's plans from outside Germany would help them in persuading him towards peace. They wanted an important British politician to give a strong speech which would appeal to those Germans who did not want war. However, the British ambassador in Berlin, Neville Henderson, advised against a firm stand. He was himself an admirer of some aspects of the Nazi government's work. He thought that a stand by the British might irritate Hitler. After the war the Ambassador admitted that at that stage, 'Nothing but the immediate and direct threat of war would have stopped Hitler'.

The German opposition continued to try to persuade Britain to adopt a firm line. Another group at the Foreign Ministry was also working to bring outside pressure to bear on Hitler. They had

B *Dr Carl Goerdeler in July 1944*

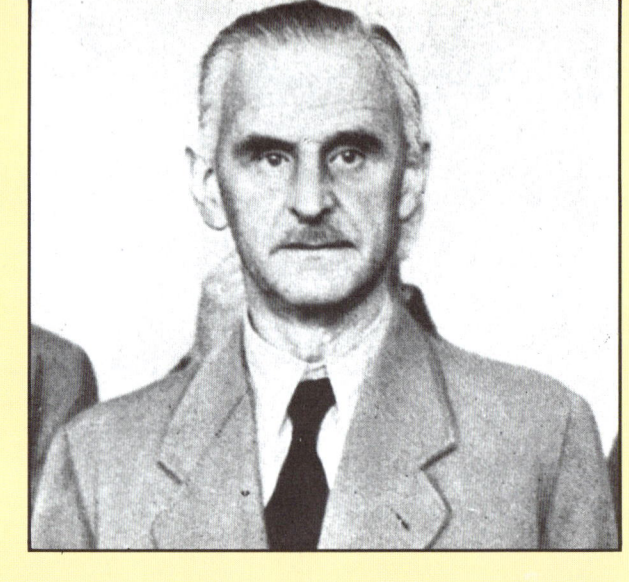

C *Chamberlain inspects a guard of honour at Münich airport before going to meet Hitler*

D *British Prime Minister, Neville Chamberlain, shakes hands with Hitler at a meeting at Godesberg on 22 September 1938. The British Ambassador, Neville Henderson, stands on Chamberlain's left.*

managed to get one of their officials in London, Theo Kordt, to see the new British Foreign Secretary, Lord Halifax, in a secret meeting on 6 September 1938. Kordt told Lord Halifax the views of the influential German military and political group he spoke for: that war would have been less possible back in 1914 if only the British had stated clearly their determination to fight alongside France if there were a Franco-German war. Now the position was similar the Prime Minister must make it clear that war with Czechoslovakia would mean war with Britain. If, in spite of a strong warning, Hitler continued his aggressive policy, Kordt said that the German Generals would intervene by force of arms. In order to succeed, however, they must strike at a moment when Hitler had suffered a major setback in foreign policy. Such a declaration by the British would be sufficient for this purpose. Britain's declaration and a revolt by the generals would be the end of the Nazi regime.

Halifax promised to inform the Prime Minister of this advice and Kordt was hopeful. Even when Chamberlain flew to Berchtesgaden to see Hitler on 15 September, Kordt still thought he was going to tell Hitler a few home truths. But it was not to be. Chamberlain went away reassured that this was as Hitler told him the last territorial demand Germany had to make a Europe. The British Government *had* ordered its officials to prepare a written warning in unmistakeable language – but it was never delivered. On 9 September the warning message arrived in the British Embassy in Berlin, to be passed to the ambassador, Sir Neville Henderson, immediately. He was in Nuremberg for a Nazi rally and was ordered to seek an audience with the German Foreign Minister von Ribbentrop. Henderson advised that the message should not be passed on. He said that he had already told von Ribbentrop, Goering and Goebbels that Britain would inevitably become involved in any conflict. He thought a direct message to Hitler would anger him. Lord Halifax accepted his advice. On 10 September in a press statement, the British denied all intention of despatching a diplomatic note.

The British warning was reduced to an 'unofficial' press release by Chamberlain in which he also emphasised his confidence in the negotiations. At the Party rally in Nuremberg, German Foreign Office officials rapidly had copies of the 'unofficial' statement made and circulated. Hitler dismissed the whole thing as bluff; his closing speech to the Rally was as aggressive as ever.

All of these international diplomatic moves were watched closely by those German Generals who did not want a war. General Beck, Chief of Staff of the German army resigned on 18 August 1938, as a protest against Hitler's policy. His successor, General Halder, continued the efforts to prevent war. He did not like Hitler. He hated the prospect of a war Hitler seemed determined on. However Halder was unsure of what to do. Lieutenant-Colonel Hans Oster of Military Intelligence was a more determined opponent of Hitler and tried to encourage Halder. However Halder saw many problems; what reason would they give for removing Hitler? What would they do with Hitler himself? What would happen in Germany immediately after they took over? Would there be civil war? How could they operate in secrecy?

Eventually Halder was persuaded that some sort of plan had to be made. An army division would be put on training manoeuvres towards the end of September and would carry out the seizure of power. Police stations would be taken over, all their radio and telephone communications seized. The SS units were all located and plans made for them to be neutralised. Hitler would have to be killed though a small group of the conspirators thought that he should be brought to trial. However Halder believed that he had to wait until the very last minute when Hitler had violently occupied another country, another 'Austria' would not do. Or he would wait until the allies were certain to respond militarily or they had actually declared war on Germany. Only then would he have proof for the German people that Hitler's plans would lead to massive bloodshed and Halder believed he would obtain their support.

E *Czechs protest at the German invasion of their land. Prague, 15 March 1939*

A younger group of officers who were also opposed to Hitler planned an attempt to remove Hitler by assassination. Major Friedrich Heinz led them. He intended to mount a raiding party on the Chancellery to shoot Hitler. This would be a clear signal that the revolt had started. No one would need to worry, as some officers did, about their oath of loyalty to the Head of State. Preparations were well advanced. Arms were ready and plans had been made to seize radio stations. Proclamations had been written, military and police precautions had been worked out.

All that was now needed was the right opportunity to put their plans into action. However all of the conspirators were disappointed by Chamberlain's attitude. The British Prime Minister was doing business with someone who seemed to them to be a gangster. Only when Hitler had further increased his demands did Chamberlain react. The British, French and Czechs started to mobilise their armies and navies. September 26 1938, saw at last what the conspirators had wanted; Britain issued a plain statement that she would stand by France if the French honoured her alliance with Czechoslovakia. Despite this, Hitler pursued his warlike measures. On the 27 September, Hitler mobilised nineteen of his divisions. Halder remarked, 'There will now be action unless Hitler abandons his plans'. The raiding party too were ready. They had made sure that the double doors of the Chancellery would be open. All of the conspirators and opposition to Hitler realised that things were coming to a head. They would have to act soon to prevent war and stop Hitler.

F *Mussolini and Hitler survey the damage after the assassination attempt on 20 July 1944*

Britain declared war on Germany, 3 September 1939

Poland attacked by Germany, 1 September 1939

- Absorbed by Germany, 1938
- Sudetenland, ceded to Germany, October 1938
- Taken over by Germany, March 1939
- Frontier of Germany, 1 September 1939

However at the last minute circumstances changed and the opportunity the conspirators needed was taken away. A meeting was called [at Münich] between Hitler, Chamberlain and the French minister Daladier. Both sides made concessions; Hitler could have his military invasion of the Sudetenland. He would not however 'destroy' the whole country. The Czechs themselves were not consulted and had to agree to this arrangement. The danger of war had been averted; the German opposition had had the ground cut away from under their feet. Hitler, in the eyes of the German people, seemed to have gained another success. The Western Powers had shown that they had no stomach for a fight. By March 1939 Hitler has broken the Munich agreement. His forces had taken over the whole of Czechoslovakia. The Western Powers took no action apart from protesting. The chance to stop Hitler had now passed. The German opposition had lost their opportunity. When, on 3 September 1939, Britain and France did go to war in defence of Poland, Hitler's power was so great that his opponents within Germany had little chance of success. Not until 1944 was there a serious attempt to assassinate Hitler. The attempt failed.

Goerdeler was executed for his part in this plot. General Halder was imprisoned but eventually liberated from the Dachau concentration camp by US troops in 1945. Field Marshal Rommel, who had also taken part, was offered the chance to commit suicide or face the disgrace of a trial. He took poison. Many of the other plotters were tortured and condemned by a Nazi court. They were beheaded or hanged slowly by piano wire suspended from meat hooks in Plötzensee Prison. Hitler had the hangings filmed for his benefit.

Questions

1. According to the extract, what sort of people in Germany opposed Hitler? For what reasons did they oppose Hitler? **5**
2. By what methods did the opposition in Germany try to defeat Hitler? You should consider how British action would help them. **7**
3. Explain the reasons given in the extract for Britain not adopting a firmer approach to Hitler? **10**
4. From what you have read here, say what you think Henderson, the British Ambassador in Berlin, meant when he wrote to the Foreign Secretary in October 1938, '… by keeping the peace, we have saved Hitler and his regime …' **8**

Chapter 12 Rommel

A study of the role of the individual

Erwin Rommel was a career soldier. He distinguished himself in the First World War, leading infantry. After the war he worked as an army instructor. Hitler read a book that Rommel had written about infantry tactics and placed Rommel in command of his personal bodyguard. When the Second World War began Rommel requested a combat command with tanks. His victories with the Seventh Panzer division in the German invasion of France in 1940 showed his ability. In April 1941, Rommel was sent to Africa to assist the Italians. He soon took over their combined operations. Rommel began an aggressive and ambitious campaign to capture Lybia [Cyrenaica]. His attack eastwards from Tripoli forced the British to retreat, leaving their base at Tobruk surrounded. In June, Operation Battleaxe was mounted to relieve Tobruk on the orders of Winston Churchill, the British Prime Minister. This attempt, and another in November 1941 called Operation Crusader, both failed. Tobruk surrendered on 21 June 1942. The news was a great shock to the British people and to Churchill. After Tobruk, Rommel began to lose the initiative in the desert war. Hitler made the mistake of not pursuing the capture of Malta. The RAF maintained a vital bombing and reconnaissance of Rommel's forces and Churchill brought in Montgomery to direct the Allied forces. The battle of Alam Halfa was a turning point. Montgomery's sound plan and coordinated use of tactical bombing saw a British victory. Montgomery's next great battle of El Alamein resulted in the eventual withdrawal of the Afrika Korps from North Africa.

A Winston Churchill, said at a conference in Cairo, 8 August 1942:

> Rommel, Rommel, Rommel, Rommel! What else matters but beating him?

B *Field Marshal Erwin Rommel (front left) visiting a desert battlefield*

C *Rommel in Tobruk in 1942*

D From *Adolf Hitler*, by J. Tolland, 1976.

In North Africa with only three divisions at his disposal, General Rommel burst across Cyrenaica to within a few miles of Egypt. This triumph, which surprised Hitler as much as the enemy, compromised Britain's hold on the entire eastern Mediterranean. It also damaged British prestige and persuaded Stalin to maintain good relations with the Germans despite provocations. Besides shutting his eyes to their aggressions in the Balkans, the Soviet leader persistently ignored the growing rumours that Hitler was planning to invade his own country.

Rommel's abilities as a General were revealed by the way that he stopped Operation Crusader. At first he did not believe the size of the attack or realise the target – Tobruk. So he held back his army. Rommel had some luck. The British were confused because Rommel did not react and split their forces into three. Then Rommel counter-attacked and sent the British into chaotic retreat.

E From *The Trail of the Fox* by D. Irving, 1977, describing events during operation Crusader

Twice that morning Rommel himself took command of the counter-attacks, stopping the enemy's attempts to hammer a corridor through to the Tobruk fortress. He drove about the battlefield, took temporary command of the armoured cars, added four 88s to this improvised task force and saw them shoot down tank after tank in flames. Twice that morning he changed his battle plan finally ordering 21st. Panzers to launch an immediate direct attack. This was the battle's turning point. By dusk the airfield was again in Rommel's hands. He still had 173 tanks in working order ... the enemy had only 144. By superior tactics and a lot of luck, he had turned the tables on the Eighth Army.

How did he do it? The factors were largely psychological. He had a personal reputation for doing the unexpected ... he also had good tanks, fine commanders and brave men. The cooperation between his tanks and mobile guns was well drilled, his tactics flexible. Another factor was that, unlike several enemy commanders, Rommel's personal morale was high. Hesse [one of his officers] said, 'There was a dynamo within him that never stopped humming. ... Without exception, Rommel's troops – of whatever nationality – adored him'.

F From *The Trail of the Fox* by D. Irving, 1977.

Rommel was a chivalrous warrior, and honoured his enemy whatever the nationality. Montgomery's order to his troops, 'Kill the Germans wherever you find them' gave a ferocity Rommel avoided. Rommel showed personal battlefield courage ... Montgomery used the brains of others, and relied on military might to compensate for any planning defects. Montgomery's insights into Rommel's mental processes enabled him to last out any crises.

G *Rommel surveys the progress of a desert battle from an armoured car*

H *Rommel in a field car before Tobruk*

I From *The Trail of the Fox* by D. Irving, 1977. There were several reasons why Rommel did not maintain his success in North Africa.

All his [Rommel's] secret communications were encoded by the Enigma machine. ... but the enemy had constructed a machine, capable of decoding the secret Enigma signals. The results were transmitted back to the enemy commanders facing Rommel. It was the biggest secret of the war. Many of Rommel's top secret radio communications with his High Command were reaching Montgomery as intercepts only hours later ... [which] enabled Montgomery to plan an appropriate defence.

However more than once Rommel disobeyed the orders issued to him in the Enigma code. For example, in April 1941, the British knew only of the orders issued to Rommel to stand fast at Benghazi; not yet knowing Rommel, they assumed he would obey. This explained the surprised collapse of the British defence of Cyrenaica.

Of all his problems, obtaining supplies for the attack on Tobruk caused most difficulties. It was Hitler who came to Rommel's rescue. Hitler decided to transfer an entire airforce to the Mediterranean. He put one of the Luftwaffe's best Field Marshals in command. On 27 October he went even further, instructing the Navy to move two dozen U-boats from the Atlantic into the Med. So the independent strategy Rommel has pursued since April was beginning to have far-reaching consequences on other theatres of war. The Panzer army was weaker than its adversary. On 30 August [1942] Rommel would field 203 German battle tanks ... Montgomery would have assembled 767. [Rommel's] main weakness was his fuel supply. On 23 August, Rommel had been promised six ships loaded with gasoline and ammunition ... not one of the ships reached Rommel.

As a strategist Rommel was short-sighted. He saw only the immediate welfare of his own troops as an issue; refusing to accept political or strategic considerations. He allowed his ignorance of Hitler's grand strategy in 1941 – the forthcoming attack on Russia – to lead him to a fateful over-extension of his own forces in Libya.

History will not forget that for two years he withstood the weight of the entire British Empire on the only battlefield where it was then engaged, with only two Panzer divisions and a handful of other ill-armed and undernourished forces under his command ... without adequate support from home.

J *One of the 88-mm Flak guns which Rommel used very effectively against enemy tanks*

K From *Rommel as military commander* by R. Lewin, 1968.

He was a patriot: he was never a Nazi; indeed he increasingly deplored Nazism. From time to time he is referred to as if he were a committed party man. He was not. Such allegations owe much to the effort of Goebbels in exploitation of Rommel's African victories for propaganda purposes. The acid test in regard to Rommel and Nazism is the decision by the men who organised the July 1944 plot against Hitler to replace the Führer by Rommel as head of state.

One of the most important acts of the Afrika Korps was to prepare dug-in positions for their 88-mm A.A. guns in an anti-tank role: 'so that with their barrels horizontal', as Rommel put it,' there was practically nothing above ground. It was one of the most important tactical inventions during the war in Africa, disastrous for the British and infinitely rewarding for the Germans. During the Battleaxe operation ... their employment in this new role was decisive. If left a legacy of doubt in the British tank units about their relative effectiveness. Rommel's exploitation of his 88s was a battle winning device akin to the introduction of tanks by the British on the Western Front in 1916; the British mismanaged their invention, whereas Rommel progressively elaborated this new use for an old weapon.

In the spring of 1941, during Crusader, at Gazala, in the assault on Tobruk, his electric presence was an extra weapon. The British commanders trying to run the desert war from the rear were usually late in making decisions and fumbled the management of their forces.

Yet by comparison with the Russian front, the operations in Burma and the unfolding of Allied power in Europe, this was not more than a little war. Rommel in Africa was never in command of more than a few divisions. (... in Russia Modl commanded three panzer corps and two infantry corps, while Hoth on his right commanded the most enormous tank assembly ever granted to a German – apart from three infantry corps ... nine of the best panzer divisions in the German army.) Both the Allies and the Axis strained themselves ... like knights in a tournament, their few men in armour fought symbolically, in a closed arena, with the whole world as spectator.

L *Rommel discusses tactics with some of his men after taking Tobruk*

M From Field Marshal Erwin Rommel's unpublished diary, 16 April 1944:

What will History say in passing its verdict on me? If I am successful here, then everybody else will claim all the glory ... But if I fail, then everybody will be after my blood.

Question
'What will History say in passing its verdict on me?' Consider the significance of Field Marshal Rommel in North Africa under the following headings:
a) Rommel's qualities as a General.   7
b) The problems Rommel had to overcome.   7
c) The reasons for Rommel's victories.   7
d) The importance of his victories in the context of the war in North Africa and the war as a whole.   9

Chapter 13 The Atlantic war

An exercise in the synthesis of an historical account

The head of the German Navy, Admiral Raeder, said in December 1940, 'Britain's ability to maintain her supply lines is the decisive factor for the outcome of the war'. At the start of the war Hitler thought that surface ships were more important than submarines. Hitler did not believe Admiral Raeder until 1942, when all efforts were put into the U-boat war. Winston Churchill wrote after the war, 'The only thing that ever really frightened me during the war was the U-boat peril'.

A *Two officers keep a sharp look-out on the bridge of a convoy escort ship*

B *An oil tanker on fire after a U-boat attack in the Atlantic*

C *Torpedoes being checked-out before being loaded into a submarine*

D From *U-boat War* by G. Buchheim, 1976.

'Clear the Bridge! Flood and proceed at periscope depth'. In the control room is a mind-boggling confusion of tangled cables, grey and red hand wheels, white dials, scales and indicators; the ventilators are switched off. At once an overpowering stench of fuel, sweat and bilge. The atmosphere condenses into wisps of vapour. A shudder runs through the boat like a gust of cold air.

The First officer is crouching by the calculator up to the tower, feeding it data on the enemy ship's position. 'Port fifteen – Go to forty feet please! Periscope still under water. If we happen to come across something to chew on today, we can probably manage with a double shot ... but just in case ... Tubes one to four stand by for underwater firing. Flood tubes. Open torpedo doors!' Acknowledgements from up front like echoes.

The soundman delivers his report, 'Propellor noise at 220 degrees – sound bearing steady – quite loud – no other noise'. At last the commander ups the periscope and grapples with its massive shaft looking for all the world like a dancing bear. He is searching intently ... time ticks by without a word from him. '... once more – an exact bearing.' '225 degrees – getting louder' 'There she goes – quite a nice ship! Awful weather. She can't be tacking, can she? Range 12 000. We'll have to fire a spread. Dispersal at an angle of 3 degrees.' But the moment he ups and periscope again he starts grumbling and cursing. The steamer had taken to zigzagging. Could the crew have caught sight of our periscope?

He spins round in a circle for a look all the way round. You never know there could be a destroyer lurking. 'Zigzagging again!! But not that much really – more or less exactly what we need! Range 1500. Course 12 knots. Torpedoes to 16 feet. Bow right – angle fifty – follow changing angle!' I can hear the calculator purring as it transmits the new periscope directions to the deadly eels. The tension is overwhelming. 'Tube one!' A measured pause. 'Fire!' I instantly feel the slight jolt caused by the ejection of a torpedo, 'Tube two – Fire!'.

We surface, Show ourselves. I have often asked myself what can they be feeling, the men aboard a doomed vessel, when our streaming tower emerges suddenly in an eddy of frothing water, when our heads bristling with binoculars appear above the bulwark ... Hatred? Horror? Paralysis?

E *Engineers watch the depth gauge during a dive*

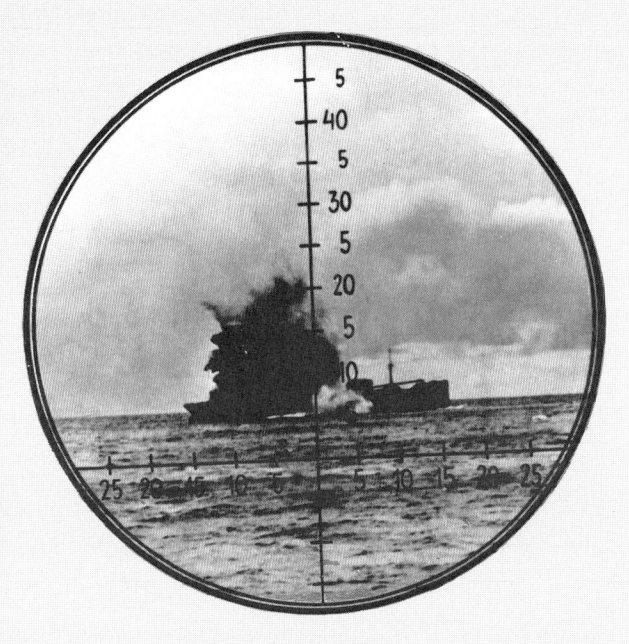

G *The view through a periscope as a torpedo finds its target*

F Extracts from eye witness accounts of U-boat attacks, taken from *Convoy* by M. Middlebrook, 1976.

> I saw under the surface two streaks of greasy light, parallel, moving fast, coming in at an angle. There was no time to shout a warning; in one instant there were the tracks, in another a great shattering crash ... events followed in meaningless confusion. There was no choice but to jump overboard and swim for it. Cries for help were all over the ocean.
>
> I was just passing number 4 hatch when it happened. I felt the iron deckplating rattle and shake under my feet. I saw a flash of light and I felt a torrent of water all over my body and then I was blasted away.
>
> Quite suddenly she sank ... there were still many icebergs around. The best that we could do was to save as many lives as we could. There were many lifeboats, some with only a few men in them ... but there were dozens of red specks in the water – they were the red lights on the personal lifebelts. As daylight came the extent of the tragedy became apparent – a very large patch of fuel oil and many a corpse floating in it.
>
> The survivors were getting onto the scrambling nets and our sailors were flinging them inboard in great heaps ... There was a little boy; an RAF officer threw him like a rugger ball up onto our deck ... he was still breathing but completely numb ... there was a pretty girl with long hair; she grabbed the net but slipped back. A sailor with split-second timing, leant over, grabbed her hair and swung her right up and onto the deck.

H From *Convoy* by M. Middlebrook, 1976.

> Admiral Dönitz, commander of the German submarines intended that if several U-boats could be gathered together and all strike at the same night, then untold execution could be wrought among the merchant ships. The Germans called it the 'wolf tactic' ... the British soon named the U-boats 'wolf packs'. These tactics were introduced in the autumn of 1940. A watchful U-boat or long range reconnaissance aircraft would spot and report a convoy ... U-boat headquarters would order all nearby boats to close in ... In just three nights in October [1940] three convoys lost thirty-eight ships to wolf pack attacks.

J In the crucial month of May 1943, Admiral Dönitz wrote this explanation of the German position to Hitler.

> The reason for the present crisis in the U-boat war is the considerable increase in enemy air strength ... there is the deployment of aircraft carriers with North Atlantic convoys so that all sea lanes are now under surveillance. The decisive point is a new direction-finding device, also used by surface ships, the aircraft locate the U-boats and then launch surprise attacks in low cloud, poor visibility, or at night. In the past month the losses have increased from roughly 13 per cent of those at sea to around 30 per cent. These losses are too high. We must now conserve our forces, otherwise it will only benefit the enemy.

I A group of U-boats underway in 1941

K Allied shipping losses and U-Boat statistics, 1939–1944

Year	Ships sunk	Tonnage	U-boats sunk	U-boats built
1939	114	421 156	9	—
1940	471	2 186 158	23	76
1941	432	2 171 754	35	218
1942	1 160	6 266 215	87	238
1943	463	2 321 300	237	279
1944	132	773 767	237	—

L A depth-charge explodes behind the warship that dropped it

M From *Nazism 1919–1945*, Vol III, by J. Noakes and G. Pridham, 1988.

The other essential ingredient in the victory in the Battle of the Atlantic [wa ULTRA the British operation for decoding the German ENIGMA cyphers use the transmission of signals between Berlin and the submarines at sea. From beginning of June 1941, the British could read the German naval signals, lo the submarines and determine their course. As a result, convoys could be diverted away from them.

N *A U-boat being bombed. Taken by surprise one bare-legged sailor stands in awe while the other ducks. A depth bomb can be seen (bottom centre) about to hit the water*

O *Survivors from a sunken U-boat being brought aboard a British destroyer*

Question
Using all of the evidence you have studied in this chapter explain how the Atlantic war was fought and won. You should consider the following aspects in your account.
   a) the purpose of U-boat warfare.
   b) the nature of U-boat warfare.
   c) turning points in Battle for the Atlantic
   d) the reasons for the outcome.

30

Chapter 14 'Barbarossa': the invasion of Russia, 1941

A study in cause and consequence

On 18 December 1940 Hitler issued the order for the invasion of Russia, Operation Barbarossa. It began at dawn on 22 June 1941 using all the available German forces – over 3 million men, 3 350 tanks and 7 146 guns, as well as nearly 2 000 aircraft. Against them, ranged on the Russian's Western Front 2.8 million troops, 1 800 tanks and 1 540 aircraft. Stalin, the Russian leader, had not believed British intelligence warnings about an attack. With the benefit of surprise, the German armies made rapid progress, up to 600 kilometres on the central front. Very soon though the German advance slowed down. The terrain was difficult for tanks and the infantry. The Russians fought fiercely and caused high German casualties and loss of equipment.

A *The Germans take over Rostov, in Russia, 1941*

B From *Mein Kampf* by Adolf Hitler, 1928

The National Socialist movement must seek to eliminate the disastrous imbalance between our population and the area of our national territory, regarding the latter as the source of our food and the basis of our political power. When we speak of new land in Europe today we must mainly bear in mind Russia and the border states subject to her. Destiny itself seems to wish to point the way for us here ... in delivering Russia over to Communism ... the Germanic nucleus of its governing classes ... has been replaced by the Jew.

... If we look around for European allies from this point of view, only two states remain: England and Italy.

C Hitler speaking in November 1939 to over 200 senior officers of the armed forces after the occupation of Poland. Hitler tried to convince them of the need for an early attack in the West.

> Russia is not at present dangerous. We have a treaty with Russia. Treaties are only kept so long as they serve their purpose. We can oppose Russia only when we are free in the West. At the present time the Russian army is of little account. The moment is favourable now; in six months it may not be so.

D Hitler talking to military chiefs, 31 July 1940:

If the invasion [of England] does not take place, our aim must be to eliminate all factors that let England hope for a change in the situation. To all intents and purposes the war is won. Britain's hope lies in Russia and the United States. If the hopes pinned on Russia are disappointed then America will fall by the wayside, because elimination of Russia would greatly increase Japan's power in the Far East. Russia is the Far Eastern sword of Britain and the United States pointed at Japan.

With Russia smashed Britain's last hope would be shattered. Spring '41! The sooner Russia is crushed the better. Attack achieves its purpose only if the Russian state can be shattered to its roots with one blow. Holding only part of the country will not do. Standing still during the winter would be perilous. If we start in May '41, we would have five months to finish the job in.

E *The German forces advance on the Eastern Front*

F *The Third Panzer Division crossing the River Bug*

G *Russian partisans being executed by German soldiers*

H *Red Army soldiers attack a German tank*

I *Russian prisoners alongside a Panzer division*

J From General Halder's diary, 11 August 1941.

... we have underestimated the Russian giant ... at the start of the war we reckoned on 200 enemy divisions. Now we have already counted 360. These are not armed and equipped according to our standards and their leadership is often poor. But there they are, and if we smash a dozen of them, the Russians simply put up another dozen. Time favours them, they are near their own resources. We are moving farther and farther away from ours. Our troops sprawled over an immense line are subjected to the enemy's incessant attacks ... in these enormous spaces too many gaps have to be left open.

K *The bitterly cold Russian winter paralysed the German offensive*

L *Citizens of Leningrad work on the defence of the city. Russians destroyed both rail and road bridges to prevent German supplies from getting through*

M *Thick mud covered the roads and railway locomotives could not operate in the extreme cold*

N From *Hitler and Russia* by T. Higgins, 1966. Lack of progress in the East and the problems of a war on two fronts put a strain on the High Command and its relationship with Hitler who increasingly directed the strategy.

Hitler to General Halder: 'You always come here with the same proposal, that of withdrawal. My commanders should be as tough as the fighting troops.'

Halder's reply: 'I am tough enough, my Führer. But out there brave men and young officers are falling in thousands simply because their commanders are not allowed to make the only reasonable decisions and have their hands tied behind their backs.'

Halder's Diary: Hitler's decisions have ceased to have anything in common with the principles of strategy as they have been recognised for generations past. They are the product of a violent nature following its momentary impulses ...

O *Hitler with some of his high-ranking officers in 1944*

P *In January 1943 the German Sixth Army of nearly 250 000 troops was surrounded and destroyed. The last German attempt to regain territory came to an end in their failure to win the Battle of Kursk in July 1943. Over a third of the 900 tanks each side was using were destroyed. The result was decisive. In August the Russians continued their advance. On the Eastern Front Germany had used 60 per cent of her armed manpower and 50 per cent of her armour. Red Army troops advance under fire in this photograph taken in the winter of 1943*

Q *A street battle in East Prussia*

R From *Hitler* by N. Stone, 1980.

General Mantteufel commented, 'The advance of a Russian army is something Westerners cannot imagine. Behind the tank spearheads rolls a vast horde, largely on horseback. The horses eat the straw from the thatched roofs, and get very little else. The soldier carries a sack on his back, filled with dry crusts and raw vegetables collected, on the march, from fields and villages.' ... To clear mine fields [General] Zhukov would send in punishment battalions. To carry heavy shells over heavy ground, he would use endless peasant women, their feet wrapped in cloth, each carrying a shell on their back.

Questions
1. 'Hitler had ideological and strategic reasons for invading Russia.' Explain this statement using sources **B–D**.   10
2. Read sources **J**, **N** and **R** and consult the photographs. What caused Hitler's campaign in Russia to fail? Explain your answer.   15
3. What were the long term consequences of Hitler's determination of attack Russia?   5

Chapter 15 The last days of Adolf Hitler

An exercise in the comparison of historical evidence

Late in April 1945 the Russian troops were fighting the fanatical remnants of the German army in and around the ruined capital, Berlin. The Nazis realised that the war was lost. Goering and Himmler had tried to contact the allies and to negotiate a peace. Hitler knew that Mussolini was dead and his own fate was sealed. From his underground bunker at the Chancellery Hitler made arrangements for the end.

A Russian troops in Berlin

B Hitler inspecting the Hitler Youth on his fifty-sixth birthday, 20 April 1945

C From Hitler's Last Will and Testament, 29 April 1945.

... I wish to share the fate that millions of others have accepted ... Further I will not fall into the hands of an enemy who requires a new spectacle, exhibited by Jews, to divert his hysterical masses. I have decided to remain in Berlin and there, of my own free will to choose death at the moment when I believe the position of Führer and Chancellor can no longer be held ... I myself as founder and creator of this movement, have preferred death to cowardly abdication or even capitulation ...

E From *The Last Hundred Days* by J. Toland, 1966.

At 3.30 p.m. Hitler picked up a pistol. He was alone in his quarters with Eva Braun. She was already dead. She was on a couch, slumped over the armrest, poisoned. Hitler sat at a table. Behind him was a picture of Frederick the Great, in front a picture of Hitler's mother as a young woman. He put the pistol barrel in his mouth and fired.

Linge [Hitler's servant] and Dr Stumpfegger carried out Hitler's body in a dark brown army blanket. Kempka [Hitler's chauffeur] and Günsche [one of Hitler's aides] stretched out Eva's body on Hitler's right ... A gust of wind moved Hitler's hair. Kempka opened the jerrican. A shell exploded showering him with debris; shrapnel whizzed past his head. He scrambled back for refuge. Shivering with revulsion, Kempka sprinked them with gasoline. He saw the same reaction in the faces of Linge and Günsche, who were also pouring gasoline on the bodies. From the entrance Goebbels and Bormann peered out with morbid concern ... Kempka lit the match and put it to the rag. Günsche ran with the burning rag, tossed it onto the bodies. A boiling ball of fire mushroomed above the bodies, followed by dark clouds of smoke. They watched, hypnotised.

D *American and Russian soldiers shake hands on a wrecked bridge across the Elbe in Torsau, Germany, 24 April, 1945*

F From *Adolf Hitler* by J. Toland, 1976.

Hitler thanked Baur [his personal pilot] for his long service and offered his cherished portrait of Frederick the Great as a present ... Hitler insisted it was for him personally. 'Baur', he said bitterly, 'I want them to write on my tombstone. "He was the victim of his Generals!"'

The Hitlers sat together on a couch in their suite. Behind them was the bare space where the portrait of Frederick had hung. Eva was the first to die by poison. At about 3.30 p.m. Hitler picked up his 7.65 calibre Walther pistol. He put the pistol barrel to his right temple and pulled the trigger ...

Günsche saw the Führer on the couch sprawled face down across a low table ... 'For God's sake,' the chauffeur said, 'What's going on?' Günsche lost his voice. Though he had seen the bullet hole in Hitler's right temple, he pointed a finger like a pistol and put it in his mouth ...

Note: Sources used by J. Toland were interviews with Flugkapitan Hans Baur (1970, taped), SS Major Otto Günsche (1963, 1971, taped), and Erich Kempka (1963, 1971, taped), and the following documents:
I was the Nuremberg Jailor by A. Burton, 1969
The Death of Adolf Hitler by L. Bezymenski, 1968
Hitler: The Last Ten Days by G. Boldt, 1973.

G *Soviet tanks at the Brandenburg Gate in Berlin*

J *Probably the last photograph taken of Hitler alive, seen here with his adjutant, Julius Schaub, on 30 April 1945*

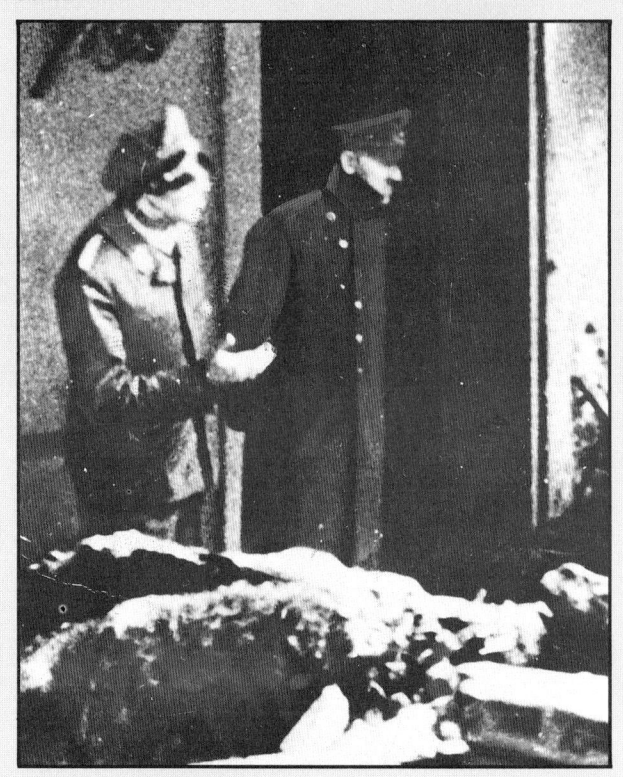

H From *Hitler: The man and the myth* by R. Manvell and H. Faenkel, 1978.

The Russians had all the bodies they found examined and identified. The evidence of German prisoners caught while escaping from the Chancellery led to the exhumation of the remains of Hitler and his wife on May 5. The autopsy declared death to have occured through cyanide poisoning in both cases. Hitler was identified more through his teeth. No mention is made in the Russian autopsy of Hitler having been shot, yet the evidence of those who carried the bodies up to the garden was that his head was smashed and bleeding. It would seem that Eva, under instructions from Hitler, had shot him through the head after he had taken the poison. Following this final duty she had taken poison herself.

I From *The Last Days of Hitler* by H. Trevor-Roper 1978.

Since the third edition of this book in 1956 new material on the death of Hitler has been published from Russian sources ... Lev Bezymenski published in West Germany a book entitled *The Death of Adolf Hitler* (1968) ... written for export to the West only, for no Russian text has been seen and the book seems not to have been published in communist countries. Bezymenski ignores the Western and German evidence ... he insists that Hitler did not shoot himself but took poison. One passage is oddly brief ... in the autopsy report on Hitler ... 'Part of the cranium is missing'. No explanation of this fact is offered, no more exact description, no cause.

Questions

1 What reasons does Hitler give for his choice of death? — 5
2 Compare Sources **E** and **F**. They are by the same historian.
   a) In what ways do they agree? — 1
   b) In what ways do they contradict each other? — 4
   c) How do you explain this? — 10
3 Read Source **H** and explain why it differs from Toland's view [**E** and **F**]? — 5
4 What reasons can you suggest for the Russian view of Hitler's death repeated in source **I**? — 5

Chapter 16 Austria: past and present

A study of the current situation in the context of past events

A *Kurt Waldheim campaigning for President in 1986*

In 1986, Kurt Waldheim, a distinguished Austrian statesman and former Secretary General of the United Nations, was elected President of his country. Shortly after his success an Austrian magazine, *Profil*, published evidence that Waldheim had been an German army intelligence officer in the Balkans for three years during the war. His autobiography published in 1985 said that during these years he had been a student. In order to sort the matter out President Waldheim himself asked for an inquiry in 1987, by six historians into his war time activities. This commission of historians from different countries spent five months investigating the evidence available. After so many years the evidence was difficult to obtain, because much had been lost or destroyed in the confusion after the war.

B From *The Independent*, 27 January 1988.

> Fresh controversy has been stirred up by Dusan Plenca, a retired archivist in Yugoslavia who claimed on television to have examined documents which 'seriously accused' Mr. Waldheim of involvement in a massacre of civilians in Kozara, north-west Yugoslavia in the summer of 1942. Plenca refused to disclose the material.

C From *The Independent*, 3 February, 1988.

> ... after a thankless day traipsing yet again through the chaotic military archives in Zagreb, Prof Manfred Messerschmidt the German member of the historical commission ... was close to exasperation. He had found nothing.
>
> Prof Messerschmidt said, 'If Plenca said today the original is in Belgrade, tomorrow he may say it's in Montenegro. There are millions of documents lying around and it is impossible for a man to read all of them or to find them. The Commission is riled by the Yugoslav government's failure to respond to a letter asking for a Yugoslav historian to join them and by Plenca's last minute intervention. While accusing them of shoddy research, Plenca has failed to provide the weighty documents he says he has. Prof Messerschmidt said yesterday he had tried seven times to meet Plenca. Meanwhile in Vienna, the photocopy is being subjected to close linguistic analysis ...

D Reuters report, 10 February 1988.

> West German prosecutors said yesterday that a telegram implicating Mr Waldheim in war crimes ... may be a forgery ... experts had found that the machine used to type the telegram was not available before 1949 ... the telegram dated from 1942 and showed that Mr Waldheim ordered the deportation of more than 4000 Yugoslav civilians.

G Herr Karl Gruber was Foreign Minister and Waldheim's boss when Waldheim started his diplomatic career. Now 80 years old, Gruber made these remarks about the Commission on television on 11 February 1988.

The historians were in practice all his [Waldheim's] enemies. The German is a socialist, the others due to their Jewish origin, are not his friends either, because they are for obvious reasons against Waldheim. We are attacked because we were not, like the Germans, prepared to pay what they paid. Waldheim is just a figure symbolising the whole country.

E *Photograph issued by the world Jewish Congress showing a student identified as Kurt Waldheim taking part in Nazi activities*

F *Cartoon by Garland in The Independent, 11 February 1988*